Contents

W9-DEB-261

CRYPTOGRAMS TO KEEP YOU SHARP

Edited by Olivia Carlton

PUZZLE WRIGHT PRESS

An imprint of Sterling
Publishing Co., Inc.

www.puzzlewright.com

Puzzlewright Press and the distinctive Puzzlewright Press logo are registered trademarks of
Sterling Publishing Co., Inc.

22 24 26 28 30 29 27 25 23 21

Published by Sterling Publishing Company, Inc.
387 Park Avenue South, New York, N.Y. 10016
© 2002 by Dell Magazines, a division of Crosstown Publications
Distributed in Canada by Sterling Publishing
c/o Canadian Manda Group, 165 Dufferin Street
Toronto, Ontario, Canada M6K 3H6
Distributed in Australia by Capricorn Link (Australia) Pty. Ltd.
P.O. Box 704, Windsor, NSW 2756 Australia

Printed in China
All rights reserved

Sterling ISBN 978-0-8069-8993-8

For information about custom editions, special sales, premium and
corporate purchases, please contact Sterling Special Sales
Department at 800-805-5489 or specialsales@sterlingpublishing.com.

Introduction

When you solve a cryptogram, you experience two simultaneous things. First, you get to read a pithy thought or quotation, and second, you get a mind workout. We exercise our muscles, so why not exercise our brain? And these cryptograms will be a lot more fun than any time spent at the gym! Plus, you can solve these whenever and wherever you want. So what are you waiting for?

The cryptograms in this book consist of simple substitution codes. Every letter in each cryptogram has been replaced with a different letter. A letter always represents the same letter throughout one cryptogram. For example:

T H I S   I S   A N   E X A M P L E
S G Q L   Q L   B R   K A B H X E K

In this code, the I's are represented by Q's, the S's are represented by L's, the E's by K's, the T by S, etc. The code will be consistent within one cryptogram, but will be different for each puzzle. No letter will ever represent itself.

To use the hints, note the numbers at the top of the code. Flip to page 6, and look by the corresponding numbers. There, for each number you will find a letter followed by an arrow and another letter. The first letter is the encoded letter, and the letter after the arrow is the uncoded letter.

The more you solve, the better you will get. You will notice some patterns that come up over and over that are helpful. Some of the basics are: A one-letter word is almost always A or I (there is only one exception in this book). A word with an apostrophe might be one that ends in 'S or something like DON'T, CAN'T, SHE'D, WE'VE, YOU'LL, THEY'RE, IT'S, etc. Some common words that have distinctive patterns are THAT, PEOPLE, NEVER, and DID. Common three-letter words are AND, ARE, BUT, CAN, FOR, HAS, HER, HIS, HOW, NOT, ONE, OUR, THE, USE, WAS, WHO, and YOU. Also look for common word endings like -ING, -ED, and -LY.

As you get more experience, you'll develop your own tricks. And along the way you'll end up with a sharper mind.

Hints

1 J→S	54 G→A	107 M→I	160 S→O	213 W→N	266 P→L	319 T→L	372 T→N
2 L→O	55 N→A	108 H→P	161 J→G	214 W→T	267 Q→S	320 F→V	373 B→I
3 Z→E	56 H→W	109 U→K	162 K→E	215 Y→H	268 W→A	321 L→E	374 B→G
4 S→C	57 Q→B	110 C→A	163 I→H	216 S→L	269 I→E	322 L→H	375 Z→C
5 Y→S	58 V→I	111 S→B	164 W→S	217 V→A	270 Y→I	323 C→E	376 Q→I
6 O→B	59 E→Y	112 T→Y	165 M→B	218 X→A	271 U→A	324 O→M	377 P→G
7 O→Y	60 H→E	113 K→C	166 H→I	219 Z→R	272 H→M	325 H→G	378 W→H
8 Q→L	61 Z→T	114 I→R	167 T→U	220 D→I	273 K→D	326 L→E	379 K→O
9 H→L	62 N→W	115 A→L	168 P→S	221 B→E	274 B→P	327 E→R	380 N→H
10 T→E	63 J→O	116 D→E	169 X→W	222 K→N	275 J→D	328 Y→C	381 Z→Y
11 O→A	64 X→I	117 X→N	170 P→W	223 D→C	276 H→A	329 J→E	382 Z→I
12 M→W	65 C→N	118 T→S	171 M→S	224 E→W	277 M→A	330 E→C	383 C→O
13 D→O	66 M→O	119 C→T	172 D→P	225 K→B	278 E→L	331 J→M	384 N→E
14 N→M	67 L→V	120 K→S	173 M→H	226 A→R	279 F→E	332 Q→M	385 X→S
15 Z→B	68 J→N	121 J→R	174 R→T	227 F→W	280 T→W	333 S→M	386 H→S
16 U→T	69 N→S	122 X→K	175 J→Y	228 L→G	281 Z→Y	334 S→T	387 P→U
17 P→E	70 H→U	123 A→G	176 Y→O	229 T→R	282 J→V	335 N→T	388 L→N
18 B→A	71 O→S	124 T→O	177 H→C	230 U→T	283 W→I	336 D→S	389 R→O
19 T→R	72 P→H	125 G→L	178 U→O	231 Z→F	284 Z→L	337 W→R	390 F→I
20 L→U	73 H→Z	126 O→E	179 O→L	232 Y→L	285 U→O	338 A→N	391 P→A
21 E→F	74 L→I	127 S→I	180 C→I	233 T→K	286 O→F	339 G→T	392 I→A
22 O→U	75 O→C	128 K→R	181 Y→R	234 A→H	287 E→O	340 B→D	393 R→N
23 G→W	76 G→H	129 P→I	182 V→Y	235 F→S	288 T→N	341 J→B	394 Z→P
24 C→D	77 V→R	130 Z→H	183 Q→P	236 P→N	289 V→T	342 Z→O	395 X→M
25 K→T	78 S→N	131 D→A	184 G→F	237 Z→G	290 Y→B	343 Y→U	396 T→F
26 Y→E	79 Q→T	132 U→I	185 C→M	238 Q→R	291 K→U	344 Y→T	397 M→R
27 S→E	80 V→K	133 Q→W	186 A→T	239 W→V	292 O→T	345 N→Y	398 F→O
28 Y→A	81 P→T	134 B→H	187 S→V	240 E→P	293 C→B	346 Q→K	399 K→M
29 D→Y	82 D→H	135 I→O	188 W→O	241 G→I	294 E→S	347 M→V	400 V→I
30 Q→N	83 R→U	136 F→O	189 T→P	242 Y→V	295 L→A	348 O→B	401 G→O
31 N→L	84 Z→S	137 L→T	190 J→C	243 I→N	296 K→S	349 N→H	402 W→M
32 N→V	85 N→R	138 T→K	191 P→D	244 M→N	297 U→S	350 A→G	403 W→D
33 W→U	86 D→S	139 M→D	192 R→A	245 D→L	298 T→K	351 N→P	404 H→S
34 R→F	87 Q→C	140 R→H	193 A→E	246 F→A	299 A→P	352 H→O	405 F→H
35 I→L	88 H→R	141 Z→T	194 V→P	247 S→R	300 O→R	353 J→I	406 G→E
36 B→S	89 D→R	142 E→G	195 C→G	248 V→E	301 U→E	354 A→C	407 D→M
37 A→Y	90 J→L	143 B→R	196 B→U	249 K→A	302 A→I	355 G→N	408 X→Y
38 R→T	91 B→L	144 H→N	197 W→F	250 Y→N	303 M→G	356 C→S	409 P→O
39 K→I	92 I→F	145 B→C	198 X→D	251 L→P	304 M→F	357 E→T	410 R→P
40 X→C	93 R→E	146 K→I	199 U→R	252 A→S	305 E→H	358 V→O	411 I→G
41 R→L	94 C→F	147 I→Y	200 C→H	253 Q→F	306 D→T	359 P→M	412 I→K
42 F→M	95 R→Y	148 B→F	201 L→W	254 Z→A	307 R→W	360 R→O	413 A→O
43 I→L	96 F→P	149 K→P	202 B→W	255 W→L	308 Z→C	361 S→A	414 M→C
44 C→L	97 C→R	150 M→P	203 V→L	256 A→F	309 I→S	362 Q→E	415 V→F
45 F→C	98 B→V	151 L→C	204 R→I	257 X→R	310 F→N	363 T→K	416 M→T
46 I→N	99 S→T	152 Y→P	205 G→E	258 O→H	311 X→P	364 R→S	417 I→T
47 G→M	100 D→F	153 Q→I	206 L→S	259 W→E	312 U→M	365 F→T	418 V→N
48 S→H	101 Z→D	154 J→H	207 U→H	260 P→C	313 B→N	366 M→L	419 M→E
49 Q→U	102 A→E	155 L→E	208 X→E	261 N→O	314 T→G	367 T→A	420 G→B
50 Z→U	103 G→C	156 R→M	209 S→W	262 C→P	315 E→R	368 U→P	421 Q→O
51 E→N	104 U→W	157 Z→M	210 X→O	263 Y→M	316 B→K	369 O→L	422 V→D
52 P→R	105 K→E	158 O→E	211 B→O	264 Z→N	317 X→H	370 G→S	423 V→C
53 T→K	106 O→G	159 I→T	212 T→D	265 Q→H	318 V→H	371 S→P	424 I→P
							425 T→K
							426 U→N
							427 N→T
							428 I→W
							429 H→T
							430 S→U
							431 F→D
							432 T→M
							433 X→V
							434 E→D
							435 T→I
							436 X→T
							437 O→P
							438 N→I
							439 K→H
							440 J→A
							441 Q→E
							442 P→C
							443 Y→G
							444 K→F
							445 B→T
							446 Q→G
							447 G→R
							448 J→T
							449 Y→F
							450 W→Y
							451 L→Y
							452 G→P
							453 P→O
							454 L→O
							455 Z→H
							456 R→E
							457 Z→O
							458 Q→W
							459 R→N
							460 I→O
							461 C→E
							462 B→U
							463 X→N
							464 P→R
							465 Q→L
							466 M→A
							467 S→M
							468 H→E
							469 G→T
							470 B→O
							471 I→A
							472 G→I
							473 W→T
							474 X→H
							475 V→T
							476 P→G
							477 E→R

1.
HINTS: 107, 115, 261

IT IS UNWISE TO CO LAIN LOUDLY

MK MC DWYMCL KN UNEOAZMW ANDIAG

about How the Ball bounces

ZHNDK TNY KTL HZAA HNDWULC,

especially IF you are the one who

LCOLUMZAAG MQ GND ZXL KTL NWL YTN

oPPe It

IXNOOLI MK.

W=A D=K G=Y
M=I K=T C=S N=O A=L U=C
h=T Q=A Y=W L=e O=p Z=a

2.
HINTS: 416, 379, 301

Do you know that WILLiam Taft was

JK HKT ZQKS MVBM SDNNDBF MBWM SBY

the first resident to have regular

MVU WDIYM XIUYDJUQM MK FBZU IUATNBI

of an automobile while he was

TYU KW BQ BTMKFKRDNU SVDNU VU SBY

OVDUW ULUOTMDCU?

Q=A S=u
h=y b=a Y=s
T=V S=W Z=V
X=P D=N U=E M=A Y=J m=e

3.
HINTS: 284, 349, 307

THe W   H   t ve   nw

YNM RETOY DJNIXQJDYC RM SQJ ONER EIT

ellw ette   t e   letel

AMZZER STMQYITMO DO YE LM SEXWZMYMZC

e tt te   el

DJFDAAMTMJY YE YNMDT JMMFO.

Z=L N=H R=W

4.
HINTS: 351, 146, 99

B P   the t   I Ph SSI

NHXNQH AIX SBO SX TCMH CP KTNBHGGKXP

t   It IS t   t t   I

XWSHP LX; KS KG XWSHP PXS SIH MKPL XW

I Ph SSI I e thet

KTNBHGGKXP SIHO SBO SX TCMH.

N=P K=I   S=t B=h Q=e G=s

7

5.

HINTS: 151, 52, 341

CUFLS IZVIJZVO, EVMOFMH OB XVD AFC
(handwritten: C ...)

JFUU EFOA V LAZLS, EVC OBUI JD EVFOZP
(handwritten: a,I C C ... R)

OAVO YVMVHZYZMO PNUZC PZWNFPZ
(handwritten: R R R R R)

XVDFMH LAZLS EFOA V JFUU.
(handwritten: C C a'I ... L=C P=R)

6.

HINTS: 243, 339, 28

(handwritten: The Wise FeLLoW CoULD FiND GReat)
GVZ CPEZ MZQQUC NUWQB MPIB OXZYG
(handwritten: CONSOLATION IN Nearly anything)
NUIEUQYGPUI PI IZYXQA YIAGVPIO;
(handwritten: Smaller SaLarY means Smaller Taxes)
ETYQQZX EYQYXA TZYIE ETYQQZX GYKZE.

7.

HINTS: 295, 431, 317

(handwritten: About The only THing THat goes as far)
LDZJO OXM ZQWE OXVQP OXLO PZMR LR TLH
(handwritten: Today As it Did Ten years Ago is the)
OZFLE LR VO FVF OMQ EMLHR LPZ VR OXM
(handwritten: Dime that Rolls under the bed)
FVKM OXLO HZWWR JQFMH OXM DMF.

8.

HINTS: 230, 7, 56

(handwritten: When you stretch Towards The stars)
HXLT OMJ VUQLUDX UMHWQRV UXL VUWQV,
(handwritten: you may not reach one but you will)
OMJ YWO TMU QLWDX MTL KJU OMJ HPSS
(handwritten: not end up with a handful of mud)
TMU LTR JN HPUX W XWTRGJS MG YJR,
(handwritten: either)
LPUXLQ.

9.

HINTS: 126, 303, 169

A real leader is one who can guess which way the crowd will be going and then get out in front

V IOVF FOVWOI SG DYO XKD EVY MZOGG
XKSEK XVQ NKO EIDXW XSFF CO MDSYM VYW
NKOY MON DZN SY JIDYN.

10.

HINTS: 63, 434, 306

You could get the short end of the bargain if you should decide to trade opportunity for security

UJI LJIFE OYD DNY KNJWD YME JB DNY
XGWOGQM, QB UJI KNJIFE EYLQEY DJ DWGEY
JTTJWDIMQDU BJW KYLIWQDU.

11.

HINTS: 400, 181, 279

There are very few errors made by a mother-in-law who is an ever-willing babysitter

XNFYF RYF EFYG HFT FYYSYU IRQF AG R
ISXNFY-VB-KRT TNS VU RB FEFY-TVKKVBP
ARAGUVXXFY.

12.

HINTS: 149, 395, 49

What a pity that people who have closed minds usually don't have mouths to match

ZTDN D KSN1 NTDN KJYKBJ ZTY TDOJ
FBYGJL XSVLG QGQDBBI LYV'N TDOJ
XYQNTG NY XDNFT!

13.

HINTS: 129, 213, 158

EPDL QSZOUW XOD GYNWOA, PD PA
OWDPUOYC GSAAPHYO DS OWXSC ZPWWOU
PW NQOUPVN NWZ LNTO LONUDHJUW STOU
OJUSGO.

9

BLMQSKT H TJZQTG SO OSRSMHJ CL BHWSKT
H IZJJ SK ULZJ OBLG, ABSFB FHZOGO
GWGJU OCGY CL IG YHSKDZM ASCBLZC
OBLJCGKSKT CBG CJSY.

SRIX U LZCXQ VZL FUGIY U VUFR ZD ROY
ZSX UMMZAN, OF OY U YCAI FROXQ RI OY
QZOXQ ZX ROY DOAYF NUFI.

VRVZ LC SKZVT PWVI KZ UWVVA, AKSV
QVKQGV IKJGY FXRV UK IWLUV FKSV
MVUIVVZ FXWRVAUA CKW AKSV YKJPF.

NSHKFV NLV EX GKJJSA AQS HFEOKX
NSFZCLCKH DLF SOKF YSVH-GEVLVDKH
QECQALU SV DFKHEZ DLFH CLXSJEVK.

HEXCPXQ'H TXQZXMF EQCJXQ: "TLSS VJ
VYNFD ILFD EQYEXQ HFNTT, CMR MNRKX VX
IDXM L DCZX HCLR XMYNKD."

HBTN "DACR" LFNW BHIFQ JOTRF

OJJDMFQIR: DACNBLDRDQU, DACOIDFQJF,

DACTQDIW, OQM DACTXRDLFQFRR.

BXLXJSW BGL BTXYWY, BXNBTWY BXSSGVY

BHQIQOXS; PQHYN BVIJWHYGIW

BGOPWYYQGO BSGYWY BXYW.

BLSLJC MKB MBXRYBVYNKF OVXRLJ TC PNZP

TNDD MBKS JKOYKB: YPNFE KM HPVY VF

XFJLBYVELB HKXDJ OPVBZL.

GAVTEAFTQ GPFOBA, GAILESZAB GR GLX,

GWLXZE GVOYWFPP, GVOLQZAQ GAQE, GTE

GWFYA, GAVT; GASFUAQ GVOYAW'Q GWLBA.

O ERCSN KOTE WUFCWSUT O TZMFZRSOWE

FR FLU KZJWOWE VZFL FLU MRGGUSF, "ZF'X

FRR TZXMRSSUMFUT FR JU ZSFUWUXFZSN."

24. HINTS: 419, 214, 151

WUMJ SKGG UVFM HMVLUMC VCXGMPLMRLM
SUMR V DXJ RXWKLMP WUVW V AKHG
RXWKLMP WUVW UM KP RXWKLKRA UMH.

25. HINTS: 257, 332, 243

VUIHYXNIL FPNSH LXDEYSZ DBJYH QUCPYX
NR FUIHYIBYH QNSJ FUQYB RXUQ EYXZ
BPUXC FUVB.

26. HINTS: 47, 337, 74

MPGK ZACE GIMQ NK RKULMKR
LGGKRLCQKAB QP ZWKUKEQ PWSCELFKR
YWLGK TWPG RLMPWSCELFLES MPYLKQB.

27. HINTS: 130, 441, 110

ANCGB-CJQHU BQQECOQG GRVVQY ZRA
FCGQEBA VD CAUREO RK BZQD MAQY BL
GRYQ BL AHZLLJ LE BZQ VMNFD VCHUA LK
YRELACMGA.

28. HINTS: 305, 370, 225

MEXW IPXGGQWR T CQIRXSJ KTKJ, HXPXUJ
RXS EDUI DC T KASSDW, SEXW MTQS AWSQU
SEX KASSDWEDUX LDHXG TPDAWI.

UXDG UBJB QJBZMPNTVA IDVVBW
GBVBZMTMPY TGDGMPY LJBDFT DJB YPU
OPJB PRGBY VMFB IPOQPNYW RJDIGNJBT.

QXI KGEU UXLI HUK GFKIGAK MKIDXT
YISFKD USD EGI, XI SD HSKY LM ST
HIGQQSE, UK NKGFKD SH MGIBKY QXI
KNKFKT UXLID.

BK EGGNE GXMA HGIEPJ ZPT NGGK MXJ
HIGEMIBRG X MTIG LPI KAG MPNNPJ MPWS—
RTK JPK ZPTI SPMKPI.

QIU PWMJ-KQQU PWDALRQU TNVT LDT
KQOWTJDF WMZBQTDQP NZZWNUT JQ LNSW
RWWP JQIFLWK QYY RV NP QBK YBNOW.

ZDN UFZ ZF JEUX AKDN IRGM VDFUS VEZM
NFRD GMEQXDKU. LKDMWLH ZMKN MWAK
LWZZKDUKX ZMKIHKQAKH WJZKD NFR.

34. HINTS: 94, 54, 198

EOB KEUO, DOGFPB KE GCCEHX HGXGH FDK

UZQMZOR KE JDK XEUO EO QWBBXBHQ,

MDOR DW KMZQ HEGX QZRO: "QWBBX KHGW

GMBGX."

35. HINTS: 448, 182, 419

JBM YMIIQU UBQ YSNOJ OHSZ "H LMKKV

YQN VQEN JBQEXBJO" BHZ MFSZMKJIV

KMFMN LHSZ YQN LOVABQHKHIVOSO.

36. HINTS: 45, 68, 259

GTYRS PL LRYWHGPJX OPUW Z JWWVOW ZJV

HGSWZV, QRS, PQ VWQHOM TLWV, PH FZJ

CZHFG TC CSZFHPFZOOM ZJMHGPJX.

37. HINTS: 297, 418, 140

EIUMDHI HRI SYZIVEYA, HRI XIAC URPAHIUH

VDORH PJ HRI CIYA DU SRADUHKYU IXI—

JAPK UNVEPGV HP UPV-NM.

38. HINTS: 215, 166, 287

QRZIC HT Q SEJIRJ QVHN JYQJ NEIT OECI

YQCO JE JYQJ HR BYHVY HJ HT TJECIN JYQR

HJ VQR JE JYQJ ER BYHVY HJ HT SEMCIN.

39.

HINTS: 274, 224, 85

NAWAWXAN, JQ AZAMJUTN TBANJUTN
WKCOU OJMA OKG YBG JQS STEQG, XYU OA
KG TQA TH UOA HAE BATBZA EOT VQTEG
EOANA OA KG CTKQC.

40.

HINTS: 119, 397, 28

CKB YRBMYAB VBMLEQ NEWUI FWZK VMBGBM
CE DB ZEFVUHFBQCBI GEM Y SEWCKGWU
YVVBYMYQZB CKYQ VMYHLBI GEM NHLIEF
YCCMHDWCBI CE YAB.

41.

HINTS: 133, 90, 105

WKVKURMEHB: AKJJTQ QDT QHU UT UIMK
RDKMK QKMK UREJJ H STIWJK TA PHJJTBU
TA PHU EB RDK SHM.

42.

HINTS: 454, 378, 12

BWZ MLSTZG LD U JPSREZ JSLMDEUCZ DUG
LXBMZPRWJ BWZ MPJTLQ LD U MWLEZ
XSPNZGJZ LD QZBZLGLELRPJBJ.

43.

HINTS: 174, 430, 302

QZ IXRAFAPR AP Q XVYPIZ DOI AP PSYV OV

OQP OVQYM QTT IJ ROV OSFIYISP

MVJAZARAIZP IJ QZ IXRAFAPR.

44.

HINTS: 70, 213, 380

XCH MBP CWYX NHTMW EZ XCHB TEWO

GMWOPBL, DHR RNP RBCHDYP ICTPL GNPW

XCH LRMBR RC ZCYYCG ER.

45.

HINTS: 124, 312, 99

UPLV UOL, AYGO SJOWUTUOSOWM, PWO

YLIADOLFOC RV FTLCYSYTLM MDWWTDLCYLN

SJOU; SJO TSJOWM, AYGO SJOWUTMSPSM,

CT MTUOSJYLN PRTDS YS.

46.

HINTS: 211, 177, 382

HMDVABSBKZWA HBCWAMPHAOQ WBUO YOMD

QZNNZHPSA HMDVABKMRUW RCQ WAPUVOQ

CORMSD RSS WBSYOMW.

47.

HINTS: 384, 24, 170

QFN OMMC MYC CLXU—PFNI L QNNILONJ

PNIQ BIQM QFN OLJLON LIC TLEN MAQ

GAUFBIO QFN YLPI EMPNJ.

---

48. HINTS: 334, 173, 383

SC MGTY GDD SMGS ICN JGZS FGI RY

VHLMYU; MCJYTYV, SC RY LCFODYSYDI

LCZSYZS JHSM ICNV DCS HU JYGDSM.

49. HINTS: 438, 93, 244

PNCXFEWQ—FMR KZF ZWH QZR WONXNQS QF

QWLR HFERQZNMU, WMP SRQ EWLR QZR

FQZRY CRYHFM ORXNRAR ZR NH UNANMU NQ

WKWS.

50. HINTS: 62, 17, 299

ZPUAHCP NYBC APKAJP UBS, MPVS TPN

TKJDU YBMP XKVP XKQPS CYBQ CYPS DQKN

NYBC CK ZK NHCY.

51. HINTS: 368, 167, 47

GFXKBP ZUOOQLOZ KZ TZTFAAH AKXO

ZUOAAKBP GKZZKZZKUUK; HJT GTZD XBJN

NLOB DJ ZDJU.

52. HINTS: 200, 355, 421

ACK TQ LUGK VCHJTYBG NBBL FQ BUF

FCBHY NEHGUVC HG NJQA LQFHQG—HGUVC

XK HGUVC?

53.

HINTS: 29, 354, 114

DWH SRCU RIIBCUJ XWABRMMD QSUO DWH

ARO XHAAUXXNHMMD SWMJ R AWAFVRBM ROJ

TMRVU WN ARORTUX ROJ ARIID WO R

AWOCUIXRVBWO QBVS WOMD VQW SROJX.

54.

HINTS: 27, 91, 388

URWES KTSW IRBB ZK UJCSGL RGK ESIRFDS

ZK URW LJK ES RGJFLC BJLH SLJFHT KJ ES

IRBBSC RLWKTZLH SBDS.

55.

HINTS: 203, 436, 392

SIRNV, KFLU ENTNAQAUC YLEH QAI TIRVN

XZIX WZN YLU TLIX LP WIRVN YAXZ PISLKW

FIEAW VIRNV, WXIEXNH HIUTAUC IXLF

XIRVN.

56.

HINTS: 75, 346, 218

EINLKSYXOQ, VXNKH YXOQAK LEXOQ, DFW

MSKWWZ EIOQZ XVH GFV PANBKEC BWXOQ

FC YXOQ GPAEK MEXZAVD LEXOQYXOQ.

57. HINTS: 10, 263, 171

ETYTYATE, CWT BKSCKNUVEI KM CWT NUGI
XGVST PWTET INQ'GG OKUB MQSSTMM
SNYTM ATONET PNED.

58. HINTS: 413, 44, 456

LMH LA CRNMI VMAJ LZR JSOLNXRO AV
ALZRMO. HAQ KSCC IAL CSPR CAIE RIAQEZ
LA JNXR LZRJ NCC HAQMORCV.

59. HINTS: 217, 455, 129

LZPJT ZHX QDUZ V QHLZIS TVJNVSHH QDRL
OPRKPTI V SVPJM OVM XZIJ LZI TPOR
UVJJHL GKVM HDLRPOI.

60. HINTS: 60, 111, 222

YWH LHMQBK YWH GBT AQ EMK'Q SHQY UMN
AQ ULBSMSNV SHDMOQH WH KHFHL TAFHQ
MGFADH, SBLLBJQ EBKHV, BL WMQ
AK-NMJQ.

61. HINTS: 93, 58, 213

QSWRL QJL WSX KR RTRALXNVWU—NSORTRA,
VX NJG J MARXXL USSF ZRJF STRA ONJXRTRA
VG VW GRISWF MZJIR.

62. HINTS: 232, 414, 76

TMGCPSYC HYY KDSL XDLLKUJV EDL H

TWCMUEUM GHYE-GDSL HLDSJP OGC FUPPYC

DE OGC PHK. OGCJ OHBC H JHW PSLUJV

OGUT WCLUDP.

---

63. HINTS: 61, 1, 358

JYKDQLGQJZ: UVDZVP BSVJK YLZQKIZJ LPK

BKGG KIVTAS ZPLQIKU ZV DLGG VI SQW

VIGN UTPQIA ULNGQASZ SVTPJ.

---

64. HINTS: 40, 88, 227

ZXBDKXD QJZ EDG GA CBZXAYDH FQE GQD

AKDZ FQA FJKG GA LDG AOO AK GQD

ZDXAKC OIAAH JHD JIFJEZ BK GQD HDJH AO

GQD DIDYJGAH.

---

65. HINTS: 86, 199, 450

DZUGSQ GD CBA DAMDXS PBAS CBA KGUID

WXH EAI MVV PGSCAU UAZMW WXH KW

AMCGSQ WXHU SAPVW ZVMSCAI QUMDD

DAAI.

---

66.   HINTS: 186, 316, 60

IGHZHSHK E JHOOYI PEBHU E PDUAEBH, EA

OHEUA DA LKYSHU GH UAYLLHT AEOBDZF

EZT AKDHT AY TY UYPHAGDZF.

---

67.   HINTS: 352, 376, 32

S FHOLWT YQHTLLW QJ S FHERLW HI IHVW

XHVTKJELWJ ZRH JVWNQNLJ S WSQTX

ZLLGLTO ZRLT ERL ELULNQJQHT QJ THE

ZHWGQTK.

---

68.   HINTS: 269, 86, 214

OW OD AXW IAXNHK TIVIRM WX CXDDIDD U

EOAI UOT OA ROEI; OW OD URDX

AIZIDDUVM EXV MXN WX CNRR WKI

WVOHHIV.

---

69.   HINTS: 445, 188, 309

BPF IRAFIB VFBPWG BW TIF BW GWTCDF

KWTE VWXFK LI BW AWDG LB WXNF RXG JTB

LB CRNU LX KWTE JWNUFB.

21

70.

HINTS: 276, 189, 94

AC KQL WHE VHZM QEM TMUFQE XHTTK

MOMUK PHK, AE CQUSK KMHUF KQL XHOM

WQESUAGLSMP SQ SXM XHTTAEMFF QC

HNVQFS CACSMME SXQLFHEP TMQTNM.

71.

HINTS: 329, 250, 452

KTEJ GJTGZJ YJDJS XGGJXS HT WXDJ XY

TGMYMTY—HWJF CKJ TYJ HWXH WXGGJYK HT

RJ MY KHFZJ XH HWJ HMEJ.

72.

HINTS: 360, 429, 215

URHP HR NRJ XBRDHX—HYP LFXHPXH ZFJ

VURZU HR WFVP F LMTP ZMHY HZR XHMBVX

MX HR WFVP XDTP RUP RL HYPW MX F

WFHBY.

73.

HINTS: 323, 52, 312

OE DWYP LPWSNCUQ QCCU CTXNCQQ,

PCUCUSCP F XOFUWTX OQ SYJ F LOCKC WE

KWFN JMFJ MFQ SCCT MFPX-LPCQQCX EWP

UFTD DCFPQ.

74.

HINTS: 231, 17, 39

WTT WVO ZKCI WNXN AZ W VPR PIFTAOPP

KN YSWY SP DP ZKZYO FPCEPVY AZ RSWY SP

ETWKIPH YA DP YSP HWO SP WFFTKPH ZAC

YSP FANKYKAV.

75.

HINTS: 30, 297, 434

RJY XGWQAWXHD EWPPYGYQAY IYRLYYQ

XUMAJBQYVGBUWU HQE XDHWQ

QYGKBVUQYUU WU HIBVR BQY JVQEGYE HQE

PWPRM EBDDHGU.

76.

HINTS: 292, 361, 322

IGOLLCKPGBJ OSN GH SB GBJWBGCTH

HRHOWD ZCU VUWFWBOGBJ OLW OSNVSRWU

ZUCD JWOOGBJ ISUDKR SOOSALWP OC LGH

DCBWR.

77.

HINTS: 136, 373, 108

BJ BT HCIMJBMIGGK BNHFTTBYGL JF YL I

JFH SFQ, LTHLMBIGGK BE KFZ THLOS IGG FE

KFZC THICL JBNL QCFVGBOQ.

23

78.

HINTS: 36, 194, 448

T C B J B V D O S D X B B J O J D J Q O J G J J O S D B W V

J C J Q X D D H D D S B J C V X D V O X D O V X C V D X

G T V X C T V J W B V D D M Q .

79.

HINTS: 335, 200, 301

N C U R K F N U I Q N M N U Q G Z K Q N F N R N F Z K D M Q

K Z N I A M D K R W R K N F S U S U H U K X U M A Q

M E N U A N C U Q F O K F K O Z E N C U

I U G S M A M N F Z K Z E F K I U W U K I U K G U .

80.

HINTS: 8, 80, 172

D Z I I D S P J D K S J S O P Z D K I L I L Z Q Q M B Z V W

X S Q V I Q S S V Z I H X J K W M F W P W W B W P O H T O

C S Q W X L Q Q M X P S B Z Q S I J F W W V W T C .

81.

HINTS: 26, 444, 83

X K V G R E O G R D P Y C Y Z O L C Y W O Y K Y Y D X J U

W O L W V G R L Z Y F Y X J U E L P D V J Y U D Y H W Y P ,

Z Y B Y B F Y Z I O X E W D Y Z ' E K L W O Y Z .

82.

HINTS: 43, 383, 305

X B R C Y A C Y I L I X O T P C W T T F J C L T I E C J T ,

R C Y W E C Y I L I T F Q D A E F P P X J T W E T X W

P E Q C Y K E A C Q O .

83.   HINTS: 268, 285, 203

W YNWVV GUB JVRNVB UGHKEQKZ QU JUAFJ
QU YECUUV YAFEK CK EURVZ FUQ SKWZ,
EURVZ FUQ MSAQK, WFZ MWY FUQ WVVUMKZ
QU QWVO.

84.   HINTS: 38, 337, 94

RLU COWAR QHN BC ADWOSJ HSQ RLU
COWAR WUHG ADWOSJ QHN HWU BCRUS HA
IKYL HA H IBSRL HDHWR.

85.   HINTS: 393, 102, 40

KR PRWPR XKR YKGA CPOGL XJS, ZIF RPZPTS
VKL SAF WRMARFAT K MAEAFKZOA FVKF XKR
XKILA FVAY FP OKIEV.

86.   HINTS: 120, 344, 431

ZE CQF KRZEMKI KZSMEN: "MY MK DGWS
EMUG YC FC ECYIMEN ZQQ FZS—YIGE IZDG
YIG EMNIY YC WGKY VR."

87.   HINTS: 408, 333, 457

ZTV JZZH RCX PZ PVQP XZBG SVSZGX DQ PZ
PGX PZ GVSVSMVG PNV PNDTJQ PNCP
RZGGDVH XZB XVQPVGHCX.

....

88.   HINTS: 264, 186, 28

"AEJ XEHJD DRZXAHMZ MD AEJ VMIL HQ AM

XYUUL AEJ VUYHZ YUMRZI," QYHI AEMFYQ

Y. JIHQMZ.

....

89.   HINTS: 178, 322, 208

HLUZX MLU XBCXZTFUY LXBF JUHLQJR RUUT

BPUNH HLXEZXDCXZ—PNH ZNFX DXBFJ MLU

HLXQF YBDZ BFX.

....

90.   HINTS: 96, 222, 107

FVWZOFX MB MX DVBBVW BC OFFWVIMOBV

JZOB CKV IOKKCB CJK BZOK BC CJK JZOB

CKV IOKKCB OFFWVIMOBV.

....

91.   HINTS: 197, 374, 10

RUTVIRYWAETYIT AM QJDQ ITVQDAY

WTTNAYB QJDQ WRNHM JDUT XJTY QJTZ

ERY'Q HYRX XJDQ QJTZ DVT BTQQAYB AYQR.

....

92.   HINTS: 141, 54, 88

GKK GJ GHMLUFJZ GUQLJZW ZQ PW ZXQ QH

UQHF TFQTKF GZZFUTZPJM RGHI ZQ MFZ PJ

ZRF KGWZ XQHI CPHWZ.

....

93.

HINTS: 179, 63, 418

"VJ DHV TE XJJI AVJBXN GJ XJYAWV

HVJGNAW DHV QTGNJBG GNHG JGNAW

DHV'E PJVEAVG," EHTI OTVPJOV.

94.

HINTS: 191, 61, 421

LJ ZYB ZGUB JQV YHIB JQVK OYGNP

WVGZBP, WOHKIBP, HCP LQQZBP, WCHTTBP,

UGZZBCBP, HCP LBNZBP, ZYB WCQX YHW

UBNZBP.

95.

HINTS: 147, 123, 291

IVK SCVE IVKCAPORHP XHR HRXWWI

AHVEJCA KZ EMRC OMRI POXHO XPSJCA

LKRPOJVCP OMXO MXTR WVAJDXW XCPERHP.

96.

HINTS: 131, 399, 329

D MGKLTGKPCJ PC GYEJV DV DATJJKJVE

HJEZJJV EZG LJGLIJ, JDMQ GY ZQGK JVNC

RL ZPEQ CGKJEQPVA QJ NGJC VGE DMERDIIX

ZDVE.

97.

HINTS: 426, 379, 173

ZRZU QX DKE MNRZ NFF CMZ NUYHZBY, DKE

LND UKC GZ NGFZ CK YQXC CMZ BQWMC

KUZY XBKL CMZ HBKUW KUZY.

98.

HINTS: 77, 109, 339

DKBO K VHDKBAC GYKG EGKVGCI JCELIC K

SKGCVTKXX KG K EWDDCV VCEHVG YKE

CBICI JCELIC K XCKUO TKWACG LB GYC

ULGAYCB ELBU.

99.

HINTS: 311, 398, 72

KPA XWUVA ANNAYKUZTN SFW PZXXUYANN

UY TUSA ZWA NFVAKPUYL KF RF, NFVAKPUYL

KF TFQA, ZYR NFVAKPUYL KF PFXA SFW.

100.

HINTS: 269, 442, 287

G PJXMP MN G VIHNEX LSE OXELN BSI

VHMPI ET IWIHJBSMXR, JIB OXELN BSI

GPBAGD WGDAI ET XEBSMXR.

101.

HINTS: 283, 318, 30

OVHYH WX XPAHOVWQI AKRV QWRHY OVBQ

YHRHWZWQI EYBWXH—OVH JHHGWQI PJ

VBZWQI HBYQHT WO.

28

102. HINTS: 356, 406, 272

HLXJ HGX BW L EKHKQ XLEFDG MDGWGD

ERG YBHMLDLEKIG YLUH BW QGCMBEKCH EB

ERG ZBKCEGDBFC BYGLX BW UKZGDEJ.

103. HINTS: 366, 313, 131

RJ HDKBRDKB D YVMM-WDMDBSVX

FVTLFVSRKGV, VDSO HDB YOJ JYBL D XJA

RODR YJTLOKFL OKH LOJNMX DMLJ ODGV D

SDR RJ KABJTV OKH.

104. HINTS: 21, 250, 436

UHKEHOX XSZSYM SR DXXDSYHP TCHY JYH

ODY XBKY JEE XCH CJX DYP OJIP TDXHK

EDBOHXR SY XCH RCJTHK RSZBIXDYHJBRIV.

105. HINTS: 343, 255, 19

CUAJTM ZBVWATJM KBU ZUMNLFMLWH EWFH

BUUOH ZUYWA KJWW PJ ZFWWJA

"YMWVZJMNJA ZYTTVZYWYC FPNLFVMJTN."

106. HINTS: 205, 183, 111

DKGHG TABD SG V SGDDGH QRVLG ZYH

ZYAH QGYQRG DY SG TWBGHVSRG

DYUGDKGH DKVX VD DKG SHWCUG DVSRG.

29

107.

HINTS: 81, 45, 419

WL IXOEFM EC MWPEVMKQ BEPSLGP OIKGM,

ZMFIGCM MOMW I BIPFS PSIP XLMC WLP

VGW EC FLVVMFP PBEFM XIEKQ.

108.

HINTS: 321, 234, 146

FAL VLGF FAKDEG KD BKUL WYL UYLL, GT

FALO GWO, VJF KG KF DTF W MKFO FAWF

FAL DLZF-VLGF FAKDEG WYL GT NLYO

LZMLDGKNL?

109.

HINTS: 196, 366, 147

XPSFBXG IPBZAOMN AP GLVG IPB XPBMF

XVMWMI AOMM GLO NVWEMI QVZZPG GP

IPBZ GPDS'A DPZAG HPAAEQ.

110.

HINTS: 39, 229, 214

KN FPM GBL BTKCJ GDJJTNMXXF PL B AJTF

GPXU VPTLKLH, KW KC B VBWWJT PN VKLU

PAJT VBWWTJCC.

III.

HINTS: 413, 349, 312

AGDVUVLU: R ONPPBMQY MBRUP AM UVHJ

LQON RL RYYAFL R DPRZPDDYP DA LVHS

DNAQSN VH NAD FRDPB QG DA VDL HALP.

112. HINTS: 246, 329, 266

HG KUO FLJ FWPJ BU CFEJ TJUTPJ BXHYE
BXJK YJJA FY HBJC BXJK XFQJ YJQJL JQJY
XJFLA UG WJGULJ, KUO FLJ BLOPK F
IFPJICFY.

113. HINTS: 71, 193, 313

I KABVDAEIB RO TBA YFT YTB'V OVIMA IV I
KRMD RB I WIVFRBK OSRV SBDAOO FA RO
YAIMRBK OSBKDIOOAO.

114. HINTS: 380, 168, 334

SNRYR TP EOVA EOR YRWVVA FYRSSA QNTVH
TO SNR NEPFTSWV OZYPRYA, WOH RWQN
CESNRY FEPPRPPRP TS.

115. HINTS: 20, 186, 146

CLELYA KY ATP GRFAT ZTPF ATP GCAP AR
ATCA CJEOHP YRDB ORL JPDPKWPS KF
ZKFAPJ MRJ DTJKYAGCY KY MKFCHHO
MKFKYTPS.

31

116.

HINTS: 211, 29, 17

COD ORR DBNV ZBPG AH YUP HPZ DPOV KP

BE OG KVAPE LNVOYABH OG CBGY BE DBNV

HPZ DPOV'G VPGBRNYABHG.

117.

HINTS: 31, 348, 155

M YLHHFCFHV FH DWL CMW ZBD ELLNH OMP

ZBLW BL ELLNH RDDP EDJ ELMJ BL'NN ELLN

ZDJHL ZBLW BL ELLNH OLVVLJ.

118.

HINTS: 153, 328, 427

NRTN YWKOQNQWK HRQYR QK NRM PEDHTF

QP YTVVMO YWKIMPNQWK QP NMZCMO

"QKNQCTYF" QK WEZ DMPN KQIRNYVEDP.

119.

HINTS: 220, 426, 279

NAWQJK HFWFQAUV DT YEF DUZFUYDAU AN

ZFWV RDTF QFU YA QJCF XAKYT CFFO

YEFDW XDTYJUHF.

120.

HINTS: 335, 409, 322

NLQ UPZN CUOPMNBSN NLCSE BKPDN B

OMPKYQU CZ SPN CNZ ZPYDNCPS KDN NLQ

ZNMQSENL EBCSQV CS JCSVCSE NLQ

ZPYDNCPS.

121.

HINTS: 6, 208, 115

OJ KRX KMQX JYV IMPUAAJ WXUZR HWXXPXW

GUBKVWXB, JYV ZUP YIKXP PY AYPHXW

ZAMQO KRX IXPZX.

122.

HINTS: 273, 185, 306

QWCWCRWQ NGWY FUJ MUD OYF QWLOZQH

KUYW RF DGW POYKPUQK RF HZCLPF

DGQWODWYZYM DU CUTW UJD?

123.

HINTS: 447, 217, 351

V CZAUVJR F YJSE FA OQGGFUHI MVGQHQAA

VUSZO CFA VNNQVGVJMQ; CQ CVAJ'O

ACSEJ ZN FJ IQVGA.

124.

HINTS: 125, 347, 458

QERFMFU WIOL, "I QRUT SRN'MF LRYF QFGG

YFMFU YFFLW LROYJ RMFU," FMOLFYBGS

YFMFU CNGGFL QFFLW OY BEF JIULFY.

125.

HINTS: 308, 252, 379

PN PA IKN WKAAPFOY LKV WYKWOY TEKAY

LPANA UVY NPJENOR ZOYIZEYQ NK KLLYV

KNEYVA U LVPYIQOR EUIQZOUAW.

33

126.   HINTS: 60, 140, 213

URH QHNYHDMA SHE TF URH FTAHWU UHNKF

CD URH WTZRU URNU DNAA NF TU EHHQF

FCDUAX DCK VCX NU FHHTWZ NAA URH

ECWSHKDMA YKHNUTCWF CD URH SNX.

127.   HINTS: 156, 375, 280

MZZYPLAKX UY PJZJKU EMDOAYK UPJKLD FYB

RMF TJGG JCQJZU UY EAKL UOJ DBAUGJDD

DTARRAKX DUPMQ KJCU FJMP.

128.   HINTS: 405, 122, 295

AJTXH DFJ OTLGY RJ HLU DFLR RFCU RFGZX

LMC JARCZ SJGZE YJMC HLUGZE RFLZ

RFGZXGZE.

129.   HINTS: 401, 9, 162

XGGP UKEYKBKU AGQM HYPKHF YQ GDK

WKHHGB BJG ANPKQ JYQ HYEYDT XF MJK

QBKNM GW JYQ XUGBQK.

130.   HINTS: 150, 59, 300

LKMMUVQNN UN ALKA MQHTXUKO QXKAQG

NQVNKAUIV EIT SQA DLQV EIT KOQ YTHL

AII PTNE AI PQ PIALQOQG DIOOEUVS.

131.   HINTS: 277, 445, 418

M DYXG DSTV BNMB FKYX NGMXB SD DBXKVT

SD UGSVT MUCG BK PMBJN M EMXWSVT

MBBGVQMVB EMXW FKYX UXMVQ-VGP JMX.

132.   HINTS: 117, 226, 149

OF OY FACTL UXXZLOXQ FRI SUL YZJI

KIZKTI GIIK AOQRF ZX FUTGOXQ SRIX LZC

UAI FALOXQ FZ OXFIAACKF.

133.   HINTS: 319, 16, 105

UORVHTK CBUP SDMZ RJ UPK QDOU-UBSK

CROFKOY BY UPKZ DOK KSQTRZKE RM

JVTT-UBSK HDYBY.

134.   HINTS: 66, 250, 468

JE JV GUJWNF HUVF EM CJVQMBHW EAH

THYZJYH HTMEJVE JY U TWMZS—AH JV EAH

GHNNMO RH-CHHS JY QMYBHWVUEJMY.

135.   HINTS: 184, 257, 166

W XPWAAO EWDDO EBTP HI W ABN TBXP

NEWR W XBBG BCPX OBYX EPWV—HN HI W

CPXO GHXT GBYRVWNHBR YRVPX OBYX GPPN.

136.   HINTS: 439, 214, 426

NKC YIML F WGBM LWIGC UMMY WI PKFUTM

KFUYL JBW F DMN WRZML WI JMPIZM

DRPWRIU?

137.   HINTS: 411, 263, 71

AEN STZLW RNFF YZGNSKGA GWT YKDNGT

BTTHKDI Z OTLSTG KO YNLW YEST

OZGKORAKDI GWZD HZOOKDI KG ZFEDI.

138.   HINTS: 327, 113, 254

Z KIERZAC ZNVQCR VD KSZEZKRIE AT UVTR

RSI NVNICR Z SAFS AOIZU AT TZKEADAKIO

RV KVCDVENARB ZCO HVHQUZEARB.

139.   HINTS: 82, 106, 424

EFHX TKAA-NWUSHXKW IKFIAK NVK NYAK XF

IANC OFAZ FV YVMWOK NH XDFSOD XDKC

NVK USHX ONEKH.

140.   HINTS: 353, 126, 418

GBJXL JR HVUTJVW BVZ FOAJOQJVW XLO RSV

JR RLJVJVW, OQOV TLOV XLO RHM JR GSAA

UG FABEH EAUSZR.

141.

HINTS: 150, 344, 379

KMMKOYHXBYBVW UDX CV UKZMRVYVRP

ZBWWVF CVUDHWV AV DOV CHWP

COKDFUDWYBXL ATVX AV KHLTY YK CV

YHXBXL BX.

142.

HINTS: 143, 459, 384

ZRN VZZL XHP DZ GBNONRD DBZAFINL

DEZAVEDK UBZW NONB NRDNBSRV PZAB

WSRL SK DZ EHON KZWNDESRV UHB FNDDNB

SRKSLN SD.

143.

HINTS: 440, 133, 290

J PBMDRUN QERCFNM RC AON QJS DA GJWN

GJOS PAHWC YNHRNUN QEJD DENS

FMAYJYHS ADENMQRCN QABHVO'D.

144.

HINTS: 246, 355, 317

VW LXM OKFDH VB XZL MGZEOX, LXMKM'PP

GZL YM AFGH UZASPFVGLB FYZEL PFUN ZW

WPFDZK.

145.   HINTS: 3, 311, 86

VP FZDG SUCZON SYEON XARDGCJ DEUBZUP

JRO NY RAVYDG ROPGLCOB ZQJZXG IZZX

OYDZ YEG YS YGLZU XZYXAZ'D FEDCOZDD.

146.   HINTS: 262, 408, 358

VTI VA YJI TIQIUY VHYSXNTZ UJVCCNTZ

EITYIDU EVWIDU UV RHEJ ZDVHTM NY JPU

IWIT EVTUNMIDIM PCCSXNTZ AVD

UYPYIJVVM.

147.   HINTS: 241, 200, 256

OCF JMF OCGMN ARP HJPF WGAAGKXIO

OCRM AJIIJZGMN R YOPGKO PFNGHFM JA

RMB OBVF GY MJO GHVJYGMN GO JM

JOCFPY.

148.   HINTS: 163, 201, 120

LIPF UIP LQNOX JPBMF, M GRFV JOQJ QS

KHFKPU SPOO SNQA UIP KVE RFUQ M GQQO

QS JOHP LMUPN MFX AMXP UIP SOMARFBQ.

149.   HINTS: 331, 429, 269

YMFGAJSH—JSQ LBA KSQ VIIF BME EBMDH

AQ LBMGI PIHHMQP EAJIHBMQP AXX BME

KBIEH.

150.   HINTS: 14, 412, 180

CW EUIQM WRT CKWRTNEXCRK, RKQ UFRHJM

KRX NEIQ NCUXEIQ RW ARCKA WHTXFQT EKM

CKBJHMCKA EMDCBQ.

151.   HINTS: 30, 435, 392

TQGTSTGRIW VEC GTG ORKE YC ILCRBM

VCLATQU KWIBB VIB IWILO KWCKA

TQSMQYCL.

152.   HINTS: 157, 119, 136

ULR DWYUOYJ GKF KUD LFC DCJXSO FQB QL

CGYLCR ZQLXCYD FXEKC CF DCFW PFJQLE

QZZYVQUCYBR.

153.   HINTS: 130, 321, 150

BKAWJA ZBJ WA NOLK MZNANXKBMZLK; ZL

PBH MBWHA PNEHAKTJWRL BHR DLBOL NEA

AZL VWDDVNBKRJ.

154. HINTS: 69, 407, 453

QCO ZJQO QP BHNVPD NBHUZN OJNHONQ
PU CHUZON PM APDDPU NOUNO JUV
EUAPDDPU HVOJN.

155. HINTS: 390, 34, 375

ZEFWV'Y BOH VGYZSFOHFKU KR B OGBZKZT
YGGU RKS HEG RFSYH HFCG—ZEFZTGU FU
RAWW JWKKC.

156. HINTS: 326, 104, 439

UKG JBPA UBBJ VITY AB PFAHCG HY WKP
LBTPAW FYJ UHWK AIRK JHLLHRICWG HY BIT
LHTPMCFRP?

157. HINTS: 155, 340, 253

TLQHPL MHO BLZFBL UH GPIOL RFUD UDL
THAA, FU FA G IHHB FBLG UH JHHW
ZGPLQOJJM GU URH AFBLA—DFA AFBL, GVB
UDL HOUAFBL.

158. HINTS: 26, 393, 44

XJRF RVB BSY XQR KSV OYCJBBCYM DVL,
OYGQLMY SY JM MJXICD SVIJRW BV GLB DVL
FVKR BV SJM VKR MJAY.

159.

HINTS: 240, 384, 339

RIK UZC PFWN GLN NPIGFXG HKUL UANMFG

YNUZKXN LN WNAR XNVMIH GZVTX ZYIKG

IGLNA ENIEVN.

160.

HINTS: 176, 39, 72

LUYXCAB SKLP LPKR AKQB—YTB KR POAQSOM

QKTKRPBZ CBQYUB PB IOLIPBR YT KL KR

ZY-KL-MYXURBAQ NYC.

161.

HINTS: 268, 370, 236

PXREJPV DWP MHCWQ YL W FJGDYGGJXP WG

IWGR WG W ICNNXO OEX QPXOG OEWR EC

JG RWNQJPV WMXYR.

162.

HINTS: 210, 148, 27

FXHG XB XYW TWXDRSFH QXYRJ WSHXROS

GPSFHSROSH UB QS BXWNXG GPSF ILJ QSLG

BUHPULN.

163.

HINTS: 117, 252, 38

XDYR RQ LDKXP AUQR GR GXT WKAADT, KA

GXFRUKXP AQ AGRKAJFKXP GA HDJNXT QX

FQNH KXEQWD RGY?

164.

HINTS: 352, 8, 119

ZQQ CHH HVCKA CJK YKEIHA FJH CJXAMI

CJZC JK XI YEKCCD JHC CSEAI HSC CH OK

HAQD JZQV-OZMKL.

165.

HINTS: 161, 30, 174

KR KU PDUR KPVDHRFQR RBFR FSS JHOFR

KWOFU BFXO SFQWKQJ JOFH FU IOSS FU

IKQJU.

166.

HINTS: 456, 58, 100

VX VK GTKX OVDDVFWAX DTM Y ERMKTC XT

GYIR DTM ZVGKRAD Y EAYFR VC XZR KWC VD

ZR FTCKXYCXAU KRRIK MRDWNR WCORM XZR

DYGVAU XMRR.

167.

HINTS: 35, 4, 154

DY VQN HR YJQY YJR BWIN YDVR VQWN BM

FE LB WBY "UQEE YJR HFSZ" DE DM Q

SBIIRSYDBW DE YQZRW FU.

168.

HINTS: 160, 269, 173

UWCKI RMIC ZWNN HR RWAI-MSUI QWC

KIZWBOI RMIGI HO PS SRMIG QNWZI CSB

ZWP DS SP HR!

169. HINTS: 78, 261, 57

SNQNTC MGX QAAS LSNPS YN BAY
ACAXYWGUS HWND VNNLUSB NS YMA
QWUBMY XUTA NH VUHA.

170. HINTS: 188, 292, 458

YBMD WHOBF KO OSZBX WFTD S LWWA QKHB
OW CSZB SF WTA MSZB KFOW S TSQF
CWQBM.

171. HINTS: 417, 2, 386

DGIYLWZY BRWMDICLO MLXBJH D GLI LE
ZJLWOR, CI RLBH OLI OBMBHHDJCGP
MWGICXDIB CI.

172. HINTS: 139, 27, 250

PXHYWGBY FHQ NHCS MBTDVCSXSM
SGSDOXBDBOQ; NVASCSX, ONS PSGGVA ANV
BYCSYOSM FSOSXT FHMS FVXS FVYSQ.

173. HINTS: 156, 291, 168

YXJDYU CKAKRZ—AOD PDCPXZ AOCA MCPODP
MSAO TXXY, GHDPO QDM AOD QKPAU GCTD
XG PKRRDH.

174.

HINTS: 96, 445, 414

BGA BYXA FHBG BR GHFFOIAEE MRPAE VYRP
MRPFNABANC NREOIU CRXYEANV OI H
MHXEA PXMG UYAHBAY BGHI CRXYEANV.

175.

HINTS: 460, 127, 234

SV'J ZXODDH LIV AOZF VI JNIV O GIID
WLDXJJ HIW GSLF AX'J ASFSLR SLJSFX HIW.

176.

HINTS: 385, 159, 352

PK CGI ZHE BDZ N XQHV IQG WGMK XBPG
EHHZ IBXIG ND XGSGLINDE
XSNCCGMX—VQBI N LQHHXG, QG LQGVX
IHH.

177.

HINTS: 357, 461, 331

EZCAC MZITOU YC P JTMRBPO RQMEATJCQE
RQ CPBZ ZIJC CLBCHE EZC IQC QCLE UIIA.

178.

HINTS: 42, 120, 214

M TALIN LQ QLXGK WEMW GHHNK "FRJIWHK"
MJP ZMKWHK ELIAK RK OMXXHP M
OLFFRWWHH.

179. HINTS: 103, 164, 415

WCADW MID BWBMHHK JABFCX JK PDT XA

VUX XCDUI VDDX QCUHD QAPDT JBK XCDP

XA VUX XCD AGGMWUAT.

180. HINTS: 284, 140, 421

WRK JKZZQH HRQ IGPPZKX RTX QHS OGSQK

PQKXS'W RGCK WQ HGTW JQA RTX XRTI WQ

OQNK TS.

181. HINTS: 211, 289, 456

EXFBWV RJRUS NMHXY SBA CQBP PBAXY

XREUQ VB PUHVR WBBQRU HO EXXBPRY VB

YB MHW MBFRPBUC BQ PRV NRFRQV.

182. HINTS: 254, 445, 288

AB AN ZHNECVBRCJ ASMENNAHCR BE MVB

UEEBMLATBN AT BIR NZTXN EU BASR AU JEV

ZLR ZCOZJN NABBATQ XEOT.

183. HINTS: 329, 416, 312

FRUJMYUJF XJ MJGS MR ARDHJM OPM

PGHJD YF, PAMJD PBB, UJDJBT RGJ BJMMJD

FORDM RA SPGHJD.

184. HINTS: 112, 20, 299

KJGT TULGR PULAFWV QWWF MXJM NQ MXWT
AUVMAUGW AJTKWGM LGMNF J QLMLIW
HJMW NM NV GUM IWJFFT VAWGHNGR.

185. HINTS: 345, 155, 469

YU FDKGYRWL QK AXYG NFE KLL AXLU NFE
WQHG NFEI LNLK FHH GXL BFYW NFE YIL
GINQUB GF ILYRX.

186. HINTS: 181, 398, 301

HLSU JFPM TUILEHUP, MIU EFPM FK
FZUYCMLRQ C QYFEUYB ECYM CM MIU
POZUYJCYSUM QFUP OZ GLMI UTUYB PMFZ.

187. HINTS: 350, 78, 158

TSGE RSC RCGHOTDOSDO RJO KEG ULA
VJGUHOPT KNRK ELHH OXOSKQRHHF
CLTRVVORJ LM FGQ DRS GSHF LASGJO KNOP
HGSA OSGQAN.

188. HINTS: 97, 209, 279

D HMMW KDGF CFRFEDFU KMC RJ CFIFTH
IMOE PTE D USDKHOJ CFIMGFCFE; TMS D
SPTH HM WTMS SADIA MTF EDE HAF HCDIW.

189.

HINTS: 325, 218, 309

WRAJOH VNJI XHQ ZM LAZHAQII JV AQXKKE
IQQGI IVAXOHQ OZ ZOQ NXI MZROW
IXVJIMXYVZAE AQLKXYQGQOVI MZA IXMQVE
LJOI.

190.

HINTS: 79, 463, 123

PKKJTXA SGNRK: U WGQ WTPK RQDTXATXA U
RQDUXV GH JKUDWR MTQSGNQ U PXGQ UQ
QSK KXV GH QSK RQDTXA.

191.

HINTS: 304, 384, 352

IHAYRIK RV XHON NMMNGARDN MHO
SQAARIK YQXLIV RI KHHC XHHC AYLI
QICNVODNC SOLRVN.

192.

HINTS: 165, 380, 222

O XTBSYJT BOK CHPT DGY SNT ETTXHKC GE
MTHKC KYWM GK GKT TKR OKR RYWM GK SNT
GSNTJ.

193.

HINTS: 382, 459, 321

MHR'Y KDZYPLDQ LNALTY YH XUHF KZX ZS
ZRTDZRLM YH IPUZRO VFVQ SUHB VRQ OZRM
HS ULIAHRIZKZDZYQ.

194.   HINTS: 369, 93, 276

RFRPD ZRWRPHJVCW OHIZUN URHPJVOD HJ

COS KHNUVCWN HWS HFVSOD KCOOCYN

WRY.

195.   HINTS: 310, 294, 443

INH GCFFNS MHI SAK MKES CXLKWSTETFY—

JNW TS TE OWTSSKF NF SAK OCYYTFY

SNFYHKE NJ ECSTEJTKX GHESNZKWE.

196.   HINTS: 387, 215, 429

SPJVHPBFQHT QL HYI BZH UD KPILLQJK

SZIVQLIFT YUG FBHI HYI UHYIZ KPT GQFF

OI.

197.   HINTS: 279, 87, 296

JLF YFQUFJ DV JLF MDUP "JUBXOEL" BY

QDOEKFJFKN QDTJZBTFP MBJLBT BJY VBUYJ

YNKKZHKF.

198.   HINTS: 422, 236, 126

LPO BFPPLX IO COWE IWDKJX DY JO

VOBDVON PONX OKKN FWO LPTE YLW XJO

IDWVN.

199.   HINTS: 249, 24, 229

K GRXMC TKTQMA MQKTIY RHU

QCJGKSXHIKM RXY IQUQYS SHA TQKMMA XY

JISXM RXY CKC STXFY HDQT XS.

....

200.   HINTS: 95, 232, 287

LKJA REC VJJY MED-ZHFJM QZ AHDKZ, HZ

IQR OJ OJBQCGJ REC DFELYJM QYY MQR.

....

201.   HINTS: 389, 82, 251

DXNUKBW WDMSH JRN BRAK LKRLOK WR BXZ

MS WFKSWZ-JMYK FRNUB RN OKBB MB

"HRRUIZK."

....

202.   HINTS: 416, 5, 394

LB BLO YABVUK YZOLK YB GVEA MQGO

ZWOZJWQLD HBW J WJQLF KJF MAJM AO

HBWDOMY MB JZZWOEQJMO MAO YVLYAQLO.

....

203.   HINTS: 48, 306, 75

SA DSPD DAPOSAX SFX OSFIU DM VA

DSJFRDQ PTU AOMTMWFOPI SPX PIJAPUQ

VAKYAPDSAU SFW P RMJDYTA.

....

204.

HINTS: 390, 274, 195

FE'R SMKU YFQM ET RMM BMTBNM OFEP D

NTE TV CME-IB-DYA-CT—MRBMQFDNNU FV

EPMU'KM SFRFEFYC UTI.

205.

HINTS: 362, 143, 393

KWVB HQXU NBJQRZ'X RQS OJRM XUWPQ EFR

XVZZQRPK OFMQ KWV NQQP UQBBJHPK

AWWB.

206.

HINTS: 30, 399, 10

VPQVTHCNQM PET KBUJ HCYT MNKT

JBKPQM—ICLTQ PQ CQUJ FJTS GCHH FPYT

NLTE P SPEV.

207.

HINTS: 128, 330, 141

LM YTXZ USYOZ ZFUZ XEOMDEM OX

KMXQTKEMCTW, CQK LFMD OZ EQTWS DQZ

QRMD ZFM LODSQL OZ UOK-EQDSOZOQDMS

ZFM ZKUOD.

208.

HINTS: 187, 322, 106

NQXXYZQTO XZEU OZEDQTO BLQTOR—

SEQHYR DLQHL PZY HFGBQSPBYN RLEFGN

TYSYZ IY ZPQRYN.

209.

HINTS: 365, 441, 234

RAM SYF FQKIA MYWH IATJXHQS FAKF FAQ

QKLTQLF RKM FY HTX FAQVLQJZQL YN KS

WSRQJIYVQ IAYHQ TL FY XY TF

TVVQXTKFQJM.

210.

HINTS: 79, 248, 426

QZMOUOUY CVMUX BVMZUOUY QFV ZGBVX;

VLJVZOVUEV CVMUX BVMZUOUY QFV

VLEVJQOIUX QI QFVC.

211.

HINTS: 357, 136, 309

HFYJXUS HFY IXQQVII: EDNGZ XT S

TYFCXQE EDSE QFIEI S CNJV EF JSZV, IVUUI

HFY S CFUUSY, SGC NI DSMNE-HFYJNGR.

212.

HINTS: 207, 287, 326

FHKCDH EL C UCAL-XDBXU LED MEB YCM

LRVQ MEB NDCFFHQ UEAQ EL XUH KDEVN

UCAL.

213.

HINTS: 42, 464, 249

BTU PUFKPDKQHU MJYTR YC MJU IKX

KQCUTLU LKT FKDU MJU JUKPM RPBI

GBTNUP BG CBFUQBNX UHCU.

214. HINTS: 110, 285, 197

RCX TCRBAV CZJ VBGBQCZ AU C

MUGWUZACRQJ RJX—JCVN JEUSPT AU PJA

BEAU, RSA AJZZBRQN XBWWBMSQA AU PJA

USA UW.

215. HINTS: 193, 145, 127

DOLBCSBSMU CXA UWVFAM OKVA SZ MAQAO

L ZLBOSISBA—SC ZXWKVF NA CXWKUXC WI

LZ L VWMU-CAOH SMQAZCHAMC.

216. HINTS: 74, 452, 244

UH WHFBXSLMP BABCR UYR XH FYZB HXSBC

GBHGKB SYGGR BABM LE LX LW HMKR

KBYALMP XSBF YKHMB.

217. HINTS: 258, 192, 462

NBUV GOTW ZMB'CT IMV VOT UORST YMD

VOT NMX, ZMBD EOQHADTW UVMS

XTHQTCQWI QW URWVR EHRBU.

218. HINTS: 51, 164, 366

WYDDHWW NW F GONALI, AMTRNEA WYE ILFI

UFQHW ONKNDYMTYWMV YENUZTOIFEI FMM

ILH WLFKTRV XMHDQW TX UFEV XFNMYOHW.

219. HINTS: 210, 143, 39

EXBUY DXPBUNZ KV GSZM FXP UBZ
TXVKWKQZ U DXPBVZ XR UDWKXM KV BKNSW,
WSZM RXYYXG KW IZVTKWZ UIQZBVZ
DBKWKDKVE.

220. HINTS: 89, 120, 384

UGNDN ISMYO JKKMDNOYA EN J VMIG
FDNJUND QSYMVN SX PSDW UMDBNO SMU RX
PN ORO BSU YRQN RB KMIG J "IYSIW-NANO"
PSDYO.

221. HINTS: 220, 38, 470

LDRN RNA VBGERHGR VBER BU JDKDGO
WDEA, DR DE NHWC RB UAAJ EMWA RNHR
LNHR OBAE MZ PMER VBPA CBLG.

222. HINTS: 65, 102, 43

HWFY HA DFII "EKVDPAYKNC" KC WTGFCV
GKQWY ZA YAPGAE "DTCCKCQ" KC FCKGFIV.

223. HINTS: 315, 94, 342

XZYJ ZC BY CMPG JZ SBJ ZBE WFYJ CZZJ
CZEVMET BOJPG VF CPOT JRF ZJRFE ZOF PO
RZJ VMJFE.

224.   HINTS: 327, 266, 360

UV VFGQM RKPD F MHFPP MVEQFH VR LFEED

F PRV RI BFVQE VR VJQ RLQFK—UI UV

GQQTM EUNJV RK NRUKN.

225.   HINTS: 10, 445, 393

YDH O WTHQ KTMFSNSRM GDRWTHIOBSDR SB

OGBFONNQ BOCTI BJHTT ETDENT—BUD BD

BONC, USBJ DRT BD KT BJT BDESG.

226.   HINTS: 103, 413, 268

W OCYPJ QFYGWOQF EWI ZN AIQ LVANQ

OVACAYBV WGWFQEZG SIALPQFBQ EWOYCQN

ZIOA LZNFAE.

227.   HINTS: 310, 474, 193

AIHALPAFJA, MXWOUX WRMAF AIHAFEPQA

CFZ ZCFUALWOE, PE EMPTT CF AIJATTAFM

MACJXAL.

228.   HINTS: 410, 381, 119

FV ZWH UYK UOWQQ Y JYSK SFCGWHC

QCWRRFKX CW RHJJ Y SAAT, UGYKUAQ YOA

CGA ROWRAOCZ FQ KWC ZWHOQ.

229.   HINTS: 385, 79, 158

PGEC G QGVOEQ JGE UO JIPAVOQOVC

SGXQOW UOJGRXO KQ KX EIQ ATIAOTVC

BGTEOXXOW.

230.   HINTS: 18, 297, 102

AZRAEWAVKA WU PTA AZBKP BQRTBHAP

VAASAS GCE EABSWVN QWGA'U ICUP

WIRCEPBVP IAUUBNAU.

231.   HINTS: 3, 353, 120

JM JK GKMAFYUJYO SAI TJO G VGNM

JOYANGYQZ QGY VWGE JY QGFKJYO KACZ

VZAVWZ MA TZ QACVWZMZWE KGMJKPJZU

IJMS MSZCKZWRZK.

232.   HINTS: 281, 418, 379

YN ZKB KNPJV EUJ FBARJT WZ AKQJKVJ

WJRYVT ZKB, PRJV ZKB QBAP WJ KBP YV

NUKVP.

233.   HINTS: 460, 368, 143

LZYGB ZAF LIBFD—DWSUVG YI UIRB, CRY

WSUIDDWCVG YI BGMIXGB, IAMG UIRBGF.

55

234. HINTS: 241, 130, 60

CACTGVGPE GC EPJZGED KAJ S IHEJSF
TGVJAMH CHHE JZMPADZ S VPITFHJHFL
GISDGESML YHLZPFH.

235. HINTS: 13, 465, 268

WVIUQWTGE XVFS UDTFDDTE QDDZ W
QVFFQG QVZG HIWYDTCQVGE XGWIVTY
YWQDESGE.

236. HINTS: 247, 405, 193

YFA BZDC QTMMASAZUA EAYLAAZ K IBQASZ
KSYTPY KZQ K UFTDQ TP YFKY YFA UFTDQ
LTDD RSBEKEDC TIRSBXA.

237. HINTS: 77, 305, 453

WPCZE QH ZEIZ RYVQPF QT SQJY GEQDE ZEY
WPCTK PTYH IVY EPRQTK ZP KVPG PCZ PJ,
ITF ZEY PSF PTYH IVY EPRQTK ZP
VYDIRZCVY.

238. HINTS: 33, 356, 149

KEILC LTVL KYVLI VREWL VWLWPJ QIVXIC
XIYO ERXFEWCQO KECCICC JE IVXIC.

239. HINTS: 110, 408, 357

VRCOH NF C KCX ZL WAEENPW ERA CPFKAO

"XAF" KNERZQE CVEQCJJX CFINPW

CPXERNPW VJACOJX.

240. HINTS: 144, 378, 456

KYTH DIBLBHU BH AWR CTIHBHU AWR IRLA

TG AWR NDJ TGARH NRYRHNL RHABIREJ TH

TKI IRLA TG AWR HBUWA.

241. HINTS: 401, 129, 150

VRJJWHEZKJDD PD BRJ MWPKVPMQZ

PKTWJXPJKB PK BRJ MWJDVWPMBPGK HGW

TGGX RJQZBR.

242. HINTS: 402, 163, 273

ASK-YNWCU: APC ZIA UCWCWGCUT ZICP D

YZNTY ZDT TAWCYINPX DKKCK YA D

INXIGDSS.

243. HINTS: 286, 457, 271

U HACJ TZZC EAEZCJ VF U EZFX

AOOAWXVHA KAOAIFA UPUVIFX FTCAUKVIP

PZFFVT.

244.

HINTS: 362, 460, 284

QLSZIOQQM BEQ NBZPBFZQ CV SEISIEDCIV

DI DAQCE BFCZCDO DI GIEJ ABELIVCIPMZO

GCDA IDAQEM.

245.

HINTS: 319, 444, 332

DXV EXQG AXQG XKKPEG GQNTXFGGA JLG

AX GKKPEPGMW JW MJPT KPTPMO, FGW AX

NXXL JW QJPT KPTPMO?

246.

HINTS: 70, 329, 81

PQ RJ SQSHCEN IQH KHZP JTBHNJ RJWTM

PEHMAP KETI PAWTMZ IQH ECNJEBI DTQO.

247.

HINTS: 451, 181, 110

C FYCZSMYIHX UCL ES LSKKBV, EIX LBI UINX

CGUHX HX YCYSKL MCHKN XB NXYHTS ECWT

HM HX'N CXXCWTSG.

248.

HINTS: 50, 215, 413

EFJY JLAUB: FE BAZ SA MUAZQK XFLY BAZU

HAZLY AVCQ XFKC, BAZ HMB SCL YAATCK.

58

249.

HINTS: 83, 199, 115

QUDRMAC YP DWC QZYWS QZOQ NCLYCP
QZC AOH DL SUOKYQI MCBORPC YQ YP
RPROAAI LOU COPYCU QD JYBF RJ QZOW QD
NUDJ.

250.

HINTS: 435, 66, 313

TW TY IBBHNHYYFSZ LMS ZMI WM VH TB F
UHZ QMYTWTMB VHLMSH ZMI FSH FVJH WM
IBJMNU WDH EMMS ML MQQMSWIBTWZ.

251.

HINTS: 69, 277, 250

M QGF GO AMAJIN MHI NUGJQIW AIDMPNI
FGG OIT UMHIYFN XMKI FXI YIHKI FG
DXMNFJNI FTG WGFJYR RHMYWUMN.

252.

HINTS: 449, 222, 401

YGZ XLXZP FXZIGK JRG URVKCI FZGYGEKHTP,
M REKHZXH AGZX MZX AGLXH QP KGURVKB
QEU YGZDX GZ YXXTVKB.

253.

HINTS: 359, 214, 302

DL PMZ KMXL NBPPAWWLJ WKL SBIJLR QFIL
WB PLPBQZ; RBD ILW FG NBPPAW AW WB
IAXARS.

254.

HINTS: 403, 219, 136

EL ZLJOOD YAFCOW GFH EFZZD JKFCH FCZ

JWFOLYPLGHY—KLPJCYL FCZ IJZLGHY

EFZZBLW JKFCH CY JGW EAJH QFFW WBW BH

WF ?

255.

HINTS: 116, 315, 163

XIDL ZKYLD, TNZEH QYNE VIYNTIVO; XFVI

QYNE UZAFKQ, TNZEH QYNE VDASDE; ZLH

XFVI UEFDLHO, TNZEH QYNE XYEHO.

256.

HINTS: 37, 409, 344

TZSW APL EZLY APLD SASE YP YSIXYCYKPW,

VSYYSD VS ELDS APL FPW'Y ICNS KY QPPN

QKNS C TKWN.

257.

HINTS: 245, 391, 294

WPYG PDPMW ODHOTE PMV LMPOJKOPDDG

BEVDVEE; VELVOKPDDG JRHEV FKJRKY PMW'E

MVPOR.

258.

HINTS: 240, 398, 435

TI TJ FWIMS ZVYR MGJTMQ IF WTCRI WFQ

FVQ EQTSYTEUMJ IRGS IF UTBM VE IF IRMZ.

259.

RNCA NM MNSNRVE IZ V EVXNZ PZSAXK NU

IQVI NI XZAM UZI VRYVKM CZRRZY IQA

MPENTI.

260.

VMC ETYXOV YS QICCU OCCNCN RP VMC

EFCWEBC UCWQYO HQ XQXEIIP E BYYN SHFC

THOXVCQ TYWC.

261.

CD JHI APM KWHGWJ, JHI IKIPWWJ APM

WAKK. MXCK CK PWGPJK MYIA CD JHI PYA P

RARLAY HD P LCE DPRCWJ.

262.

LCHZF HZ EAF NME CD IFEEHOI YANE KCX

YNOE RK MNHZHOI KCXM FKFRMCY HOZEFNG

CD EAF MCCD.

263.

FKT REJFTJF QAJJHINT GEZ RAO ZAY FA

JFEOF E RHOT HJ FA OYI FGA AQQAJHDS

AQHDHADJ FASTFKTO.

264.

HINTS: 278, 406, 466

MEVMIC RNEQ INPU RGMQ GUGZO, KPO KG

HGUI ZMUGXPE ON RMHG INPU BNCG MO M

XUFGBQEI EGHGE.

265.

HINTS: 224, 102, 30

HJGA EMOWFC MO TQFEMQZ VJARMOAPK

EDAQ HF OVAIT KFGJ CMQW, IQW EDAQ HF

CMQW KFGJ OVAARD.

266.

HINTS: 364, 124, 419

CYM KTRC RMZVTPR HZTGDMK VW CYM XTZDL

KVAYC YIEM GMMW EMZJ MIRVDJ RTDEML

XYMW VC XIR I RKIDD TWM.

267.

HINTS: 2, 61, 218

VN ILJ CXRZ ZGH CLQUE ZL AHXZ X MXZG

ZL ILJQ NQLRZ ELLQ, UVH ELCR ZL ZXPH X

RXM, LQ ZQI ZL ZXPH X AXZG.

268.

HINTS: 400, 264, 188

XYFMEN GOM QMXG MRYDCGVWZ VX GOCG

WQGCVZMR MZRMCHWFVZS GW MCFZ C

EVHVZS.

269. HINTS: 58, 292, 370

GNQQDGG VG OKD ZOOZVREDRO JA FKZO

CJN FZRO FKVHD CJN ZWD GOVHH VR OKD

EJJX AJW VO.

270. HINTS: 267, 12, 76

LV JGX QGPX VLJQ, MXYO LJ—AZNXQQ BPA

YOX Y MPHYZ. JGXZ, PV WPAOQX, BPA MLNN

MYZJ Y QLDX QHYNNXO.

271. HINTS: 106, 27, 72

G PHTS H PKJFP DGZAX HZS OSJSZNKX—UPS

ANTS DZGJOX LSHFS, UPS XUNZC DZGJOX

UHY SYSILUGNJX.

272. HINTS: 376, 115, 337

JBPZ MLANO EVL BWF YLOQKQIF BWF

WFBAAZ JQOKBNFP BK KVF KLY LM KVFQW

ILQDFO.

273. HINTS: 228, 84, 119

NIDF JRVSTFYQ WFY LFIUVQL DH URYQ NIDF

TWDLRCYF ZCWFCZ HDCCVQL IQ SVHZCVJA

WQT NIDF ZIQ ZCWFCZ UVHVQL VC IKK.

274. HINTS: 160, 43, 200

CSGDRVZBT GJMJEN YZTRD PSW QSEMRG CSQ ZEPUCJEN HJIIRM QJUC CZP BSWIM VR DS CZGM.

275. HINTS: 440, 149, 413

ACI KAOOEDQI JPWJCUJHI UIQIWEOEAC TJO AWIZ J HAAP DAAB EO UTJU USA KIAKQI VJC VXZQ XK SEUT EU.

276. HINTS: 153, 230, 269

CQXMQUK QE OLEEQATK USI LMI USQMX USRU PRMMLU IJIY AI OYIEIYJIC QM RTPLSLT.

277. HINTS: 206, 467, 329

QM SRINJV DCIWVJ NCH GDRED CXRWI XJVSWHC LNRVIL LNJ KJVF ZQGJZF ERWZH NCKJ HRDJ XJIIJV EQIN INJ SCZJ GDJJ.

278. HINTS: 121, 272, 35

DHQJSTDOP JDJQIR PQQH XC TDJQ MCY HETM XMQR HEPX GDR ZCJ PCHQXMSOF XMQR YDOX, DP ICOF DP SX SP OCX DII DX COTQ.

279.   HINTS: 152, 105, 223

YKOSGYQ PSGB PK OKGTTF LKKU CL BSKQK

KVBOKJKTF SKDBCD UGFQ CQ G

"DGTJYTKV."

280.   HINTS: 304, 205, 409

I MPPBFIVV LPILQ'D BPZSQGDB WOPFVGYD

IOG I SPPE EGMGUDCRG BGIY IUE

PMMGUDCRG IVZYUC.

281.   HINTS: 11, 422, 260

YODMC GNBMOBV PIOYNY POC DMCJ PLBDJ

YIJU; HDMN PBJPWNBS, DMPELVDMR PJYCES

PIDMO PJHHNN PLUY, RNC PIDUUNV,

PBOPWNV, GLYCNV.

282.   HINTS: 247, 384, 413

ZWN GASN FWNNSHRKONYY BOI JAAI WRGAS

ZWBZ UY RYNI, ZWN GASN AH UZ SNGBUOY.

283.   HINTS: 293, 421, 351

OQF NGQCECTO EGR E IQSNTRPR JFIIRJJ HY

OQF QUV PZR PHVHRJP IEG EVW PZR SQJP

NQURGYFT SQURG HV PZR VRHLZCQGZQQW.

65

284.

HINTS: 442, 327, 352

IHAY UFG QY HDIG F PWYUTPFI EYFPXTHD,

QVX TX ZVEY TZ MVD XEGTDK XH NTZPHAYE

XWY ETKWX MHEUVIF.

285.

HINTS: 212, 392, 252

FSO NFSEUAGZOA GFTIN WIHZ GWZ

TJAITHIEGIUZ FY WIHJEU GFF CIEN

ITHIEGIUZA.

286.

HINTS: 377, 26, 234

ACXIY IYFIY KI IYYKFP EAKFPI DI EAYW DXY,

UGE BCKFP EAKFPI DI EAYW CGPAE EC UY

BCFY.

287.

HINTS: 235, 16, 39

P SWWV YPT KF FKYKMPB UW UXP—LWB GKF

BXPM FUBXTSUG FGWZF ZGXT GX LKTVF

GKYFXML KT GWU ZPUXB.

288.

HINTS: 202, 65, 358

ECFVCN RM BNGTVYN OV DMN VDQ CNB

GEBC YVBNQ RP OXNF JV CVO OEHN RO

VDO VP VDQ LETHFEQJ.

289.

HINTS: 142, 440, 266

GZC ARBG KTBNRSMJETXE GZTXE YZCX IRS

MCJNZ ATKKPC JEC TB MCJPPI JPP GZRBC

ICJMB ERXC GR YJTBG.

290.

HINTS: 189, 44, 126

MKO JGDOVM BJ UCC LGJMV UABIDY UDH

XKAGVMPUV MAOO—MKO TAOVODXO BJ U

LCBZGDL JUPGCH UCC ZAUTTOY IT GD OUXK

BMKOA.

291.

HINTS: 270, 206, 158

FO IYRT YS YL DR YKHALLYGYZYSE IAN D

HONLAR SA GOPYR SA ZODNR LAKOSCYRP

CO SCYRWL CO DZNODTE WRAFL.

292.

HINTS: 9, 238, 188

KW GWRDX EWR ICBQG BDWRX XIC VQPS

NCHHWT TIW ZBHHCG IPL ZBQ "NHBXXCQE"

DCZBRLC PX VWX IPS KWTICQC.

293.

HINTS: 178, 420, 336

"VZ GUZ HD P GUUBGNPFJ, RUI," DPHK BXM

LPWVMW BU BXM FHBZ LUNJD. "ZMD DHW, H

VPJM XPZ IXHNM BXM DUR DXHRMD."

294.

HINTS: 373, 81, 285

PGD WUNIUMPCSHD PDNTDMCPAMD UI C

GUND BX AXACHHZ NCBKPCBKDJ SZ PGD

WUUH GDCJX CKJ VCMN GDCMPX UI PGUXD

VGU JVDHH PGDMD.

295.

HINTS: 191, 230, 208

L CRTU RQQRGUBFVUO ELF TXCPRY HX

GXUGVXAXP HXELBTX UKX EKLFEXT LGX UKLU

TRYX LCXGU QXGTRF KLT LCGXLPO

PVTERAXGXP VU.

296.

HINTS: 137, 367, 106

XU QFKL IFRUO QAU'K "KTGTS STIK,"

WAJNTWK LNA HXOOAKL WJFHGAQ ZTK

GFPTLXUO AUFRON GALLRPA LF OF ZXLN

LNA LFQTLFAK.

297.

HINTS: 237, 419, 282

ZA-ZMCCMU: I VMURAW PYA MWCMUR IDCMU

XAF QW I UMJANJQWZ LAAU IWL PQWLR FV

PIX IYMIL AD XAF.

298.   HINTS: 55, 43, 76

GJAMVUK, NLMHU NII JA ANJC NDC CVDH,
JA VDIK BVAAJS ZGJEG GNSSHDA MV BUVZ
VIC BUNEHLTIIK.

299.   HINTS: 16, 183, 401

GQQGNUSPMUI AYI XPGBX; KGZDLDN,
UDAQUYUMGP SRSYFFI XMBXR UKD OGGN
OGZP.

300.   HINTS: 390, 442, 287

K PNFCQ'A QLAPXFZUFEW EI K NEULC: K
ZCKPL JEV AUKJ KU FI JEV NKBL WE
XLCKUFBLA.

301.   HINTS: 423, 383, 448

CIX ECINXTHSD JOAIK GYCSJ VCIHCTPAJZ—
ZCS PGZ FTGVJAVX AJ EAJOCSJ YXAIK
VCIQFAVSCSQ.

302.   HINTS: 22, 152, 310

FRMTYPYRG PV: "VQOKIFOU TIQY WRXFK
YOU OY DQG DPTU TPAR; QMFRG XF P WXK
IQAR."

303.   HINTS: 369, 100, 329

DTGJ TZK DNBIFZJ ESOO VGSOJ NZ IPJ GTZ
EPN HTZ HNZIBSMJ IN SZMJZI IJTBUBNND
NZSNZ UJJOJBV.

304.   HINTS: 92, 26, 398

CY ILZS, LI CY OYTFAY IFBO MYGGYOU IOFT
GEY CFOS "WBYBY," CY UGLMM HOFZFBZDY
LG "W." EFC HYDBMLPO!

305.   HINTS: 1, 137, 15

JOMMHJJ RJQ'L EIUEPJ VRQEI. RV PNO
ZORIA E ZHLLHF KNOJHLFEX, QELOFH URII
ZFHHA E JKEFLHF KNOJH.

306.   HINTS: 306, 239, 319

DSAE GPE ND NG VADDAZ, VE LPZ, DC SPWA
TCWAM P GSCZD LATTCY DSPO OAWAZ DC
SPWA TCWAM P DPTT.

307.   HINTS: 192, 326, 467

LEZS KUG KXSG ZL R MRKMU RQT KUG
KGCCXQD ZL XK, R LXVU ZLKGQ XQMEGRVGV
RSRAXQDCI XQ VXAG.

70

308. HINTS: 79, 426, 93

SBUG NRXNMR YRMFRCR IRUFWO QX YR B

LRERHFQBEG QLFUI; QLXOR DLX QLFUZ

XQLREDFOR SWOQ JREQBFUMG LBCR UX

JLFMHERU.

---

309. HINTS: 288, 475, 453

VPP RSHF YUTHGTO HUT UDDIHV VFI

FIUNV—UTY LGVVGTO PSV VPP RUTQ GLT'V

OPPY DPN GV, IGVFIN.

---

310. HINTS: 113, 311, 287

BNRL XEX XEXXRQ XEXKEGL, ZM XEXXRQ AE

NCGQ MNCM ZM XEXXRQ ZLME XEX'A

XEKDRM, SLMZJ XEX'A XEKDRM JEEDRQ JZDR

C XEKDRM MNCM BESJQ XEX.

---

311. HINTS: 271, 419, 252

MEBMLXMHNM XA U OULC KMUNOML. AOM'A

KOM QHFG QHM TOQ BLMAMHKA KOM KMAK

IXLAK UHC KOM FMAAQH UIKMLTULC.

71

312.   HINTS: 245, 163, 344

KQYIZKT SCEVL ML RCO MR RCLY XMV
XVKYZLY WZDDL ZK TAVCY IMAAO DZEV
YIAQWWZKT YQQYICFIVL.

313.   HINTS: 216, 358, 241

GW EVT QSSVY EVTZ NGHO CV CDGPN LVPXE
KZVYO VP CZXXO, OVLXHQE CDXE JVTSH KXC
JQTKDC VTC VP Q SGLF.

314.   HINTS: 372, 55, 406

CEG MGNIUT SNTV SGT BUIG NT NMXKSGTC
RDCE NT NBNMS LBULW DI JGLNKIG CEGV
CNWG DC BVDTX HURT.

315.   HINTS: 137, 166, 117

HL'F J UTIPYHJE LMHXB JRNPL YHCT—HC
QNP JRFNYPLTYQ ETCPFT LN JIITUL
JXQLMHXB RPL LMT RTFL, QNP NCLTX BTL
HL.

316.   HINTS: 364, 437, 230

EF XRADM G KTZIYD EXZMIU AU'R DTJ
OTRRAEVI BTY UJT OITOVI UT MT ADUT ZIEU
RFRUIKGUAHGVVF.

72

317.

HINTS: 204, 294, 159

RZ AUY UVH P QUI, KUB'I VUOOA, ZUO

HXHB IJH GROKE JPXH GRQQE PBK IJHA'OH

ERBDRBD IJHRO JHPOIE UYI.

318.

HINTS: 124, 427, 295

XTMLALRF, NKQ TXBR NKCXJ CSETGNLXN NT

EIN LFCAQ VTG TXQ'F TBA LJQ CF LBB

NKTIJKN TV GQNCGQSQXN.

319.

HINTS: 116, 332, 28

MADJ FAD OEH ODEE VJFU FAD QYGQYEYND

BYG AD MYR UTDGADYGN RYHVJZ, "BXRF

AUM NVN V DTDG ZDF VJFU FAVR BYQ?"

320.

HINTS: 64, 378, 8

UHQK EVQQ: PJNM V FZLB NTVQQ HEPZRM

AWXRW LZTVXIN HI MWZ MZZ AWXQZ V

GZLNGXLXIU WJTVI KVIN XM FXUHLHJNQB

AXMW V QHIU RQJE.

321.

HINTS: 22, 178, 119

GIC AUOM RUEZ QLRQ. AUO SEA BUC MIENQ

LC, KOC AUO'ZZ WOC UB SOGNZI NZLSKLBR

OWFEMT CUFEMT LC.

322.   HINTS: 436, 274, 421

AX'Z UPHNROG BQZZALOC KQF N BCFZQR

XQ SQ N XFCHCRSQPZ NHQPRX QK ONLQF—

XUNX AZ, AK AX'Z RQX XUC XUARE UC'Z

ZPBBQZCS XQ LC SQARE.

323.   HINTS: 46, 173, 220

DIUCOPN DI XG ONXFG KIN MNXLGE OXCPM

NXWM UXE. DH IKGMDIP HCIIDNL WKTNF

XOKIP, OXCPM XG EKCLFNOH.

324.   HINTS: 135, 263, 158

CMOTO UZ KI TOLZIK CI YLPO CMO ZLYO

YUZCLPO CXUAO XMOK CMOTO LTO ZI YLKB

ICMOTZ CI YLPO.

325.   HINTS: 213, 174, 232

KL GDT UXE U FBKYS LDH RBV RHTRB, LKWS

U BUWSG FBUKH RD XKWE KWRD. GDT ZKYY

PVR KR—UWS WKWV RKCVX DTR DL RVW KR

ZKYY LYDDH GDT.

74

326.

HINTS: 140, 30, 188

WIGCDFXUG DVU KOC SQ ZWOV KDCR CW
ESQP WOC JRUCRUV ZWO VUDXXZ JDQCUP D
FUVCDSQ CRSQN WV SE ZWO LOGC
CRWONRC ZWO PSP.

327.

HINTS: 371, 179, 45

EJ OJFDEY D SDWCAVP SODFY ZNUE FAWFOY
ERY IOJFC DVM LJN'OO NUNDOOL UYY ERY
FDW DRYDM SNOOAVP AVEJ AE.

328.

HINTS: 349, 269, 369

Q ZIKIY SYXL XSPMF FNI KIYW SQL CQDN Q
TXFTN, SMF DFQOO Q DII ZP YIXDPZ CPY
TXYYWQZL FNIR NPRI FNYPMLN FNI XOOIWD.

329.

HINTS: 69, 390, 418

FP'N POA EFVS KB NKVX WKG NFVX MVS POA
BUFAVSRW NZFRA WKG TAMU POMP ZMEAN
POA NGVNOFVA.

330.

HINTS: 338, 428, 322

VQODQPG FC DLHD ILFVL THRGC QC DLFAR
IG IFOO OFRG CJTGDLFAE CDPHAEG ILGA IG
RAJI IG IJA'D.

331.

HINTS: 99, 302, 408

GAL HFIASAOATKC PEF SWX SF HIUTCU

URUWXGFMX TS FKOU TWU IANU T HDH

SWXAKL SF VFIIFP VFDW NAMC TS SEU CTZU

SAZU.

332.

HINTS: 132, 41, 344

FQUXC UX YNC PIURUYA YQ YPRE IVUZNYRA

PKM GRTCKYRA HNURC YNC QYNCV GCRRQH

UX FPAUKZ YNC HPUYCV.

333.

HINTS: 359, 76, 295

VODGLVY SGO HLRGYGBCH EORQPOY L

NQQH KLPXWZ HQN EORLBYO LWW SGO

POPEODY QK SGO KLPXWZ RLC VLS GXP LS

SGO YLPO SXPO.

334.

HINTS: 320, 210, 44

DV XDKHYFUME BJH XFHYIYXGNHN AHCHH

XP BYRPPUI MXGRNRVK UB CXXWK CUWH RCC

BJH PXYAHY DRIWKHRB NYUFHYK PUMRCCV

EXB BJHUY XGM IRYK.

335.   HINTS: 403, 289, 150

ZXVTFNVE, FCJXFWQCBB HA XJC, GXB ICCK
XVVXNKCW NA X MCFBHK WHCB KHV RTWJC,
ITV BNZMQE QCXFKB VH TKWCFBVXKW XKW
CKRHE MCHMQC.

336.   HINTS: 354, 204, 121

WJPS ANRUG'H DJEZOJ: "...EIG DUOEHO,
UPJG, DKX YRXESRIH RI ANOJJZ DRO EIG
RAO AJOES RIHXOEG PW APG-URYOJ PRU.
ESOI."

337.   HINTS: 101, 357, 176

F IVH VA F OTHEER OYYT YIZ ABLAEVEBEH
WYT EPH ETBEP, LBE EPH YUIR YUH AY WFT
ZVAGYMHTHZ.

338.   HINTS: 324, 251, 383

VCOM LMCLYM VMYWCO IZAM XIMRU CFJ
CLRJRCJV, XIMB TGVX FMZU FIZXMAMU
TGOSYM IZLLMJV XC SM RJ VXBYM.

339.   HINTS: 262, 181, 284

WQ'E YKNDYXDSZK IPR NGBI VGT APG BDT

LKQ ZDGLIWTL DQ APGY PRT CDEECPYQ

CWBQGYK SKVPYK YKDZWUWTL QIDQ'E RIDQ

APG ZPPX ZWXK.

340.   HINTS: 308, 63, 396

JPA VAETAZU GBH UJ WBQA B YJPM XUJEH

XLJEU DX UJ XUBEU UAYYDPM DU WAAQYH

UJ B UEBTTDZ ZJV.

341.   HINTS: 275, 326, 205

DKGMG HN E SEND JHLLGMGIXG HI TGHIO

VWGI-CHIJGJ EIJ KESHIO E WGMLGXDRB

GCWDB KVRG HI VIG'N KGEJ.

342.   HINTS: 116, 246, 366

F KMFJN JFV BGMMGAOCU QGP OY GBVDC

KFX MPJN XDWDCXOCU PWGC ASDVSDE

QGP'ED F TFC GE F TGPYD.

343.   HINTS: 196, 429, 413

SOCAVBHMAXY FSO VMZO OFSHQRBFZOY. MU

HQOJ ACOSHBSX DBIQ HQFH MY UFBVHJ

HQOJ WOYHSAJ DBIQ HQFH MY PAAW.

344.

HINTS: 78, 156, 248

ZEVKF XVMEVF DU XDMJKO KOMWVRI:
ZKFWVE KOO OJUV'X OVKHVX JS XTEJSZ,
JFX UODAVEX JS XPRRVE, JFX UEPJF JS
KPFPRS.

345.

HINTS: 87, 407, 26

QXIWJAK EYRYW BYYDB BZYYAYW AXIE ZXYE
YEAYWYM JE YUYDOAJFEB QFHSDE FT
JEQFDY AIU WYASWE.

346.

HINTS: 73, 35, 127

FIQIEW FPSSAK: HSKHQK TEYA FIEBL,
QUEMAT BCIEAF, RMSZP VMUA, ULQZX DSAQI
KEQI. DSUFV BUSHL YEA.

347.

HINTS: 463, 329, 358

TPIMGJMHILQ RIUJBF LVWNBJGJR
UVMGF-FIMK KIRZ, RLVMOXA EOXXOXA
GVPLZKVEX UVM ZVWJ GJIW.

348.

HINTS: 432, 90, 401

MP MY PAF WGTTGX EGXBFZ GN UJJ TFX AGE
UTGXH YG TUXD TMJJMGXY GN NUWFY PAFZF
YAGKJB RF XGXF UJMVF.

349.

HINTS: 468, 4, 220

PSSJGMDLX KJ GHRHPGSWHGR PK
LJGKWOHRKHGL TLDYHGRDKZ, KWH SWDSPXJ
IDGH OPR QHADHYHM KJ WPYH RKPGKHM DL
P GDJKJTR MDSH XPEH.

350.

HINTS: 258, 136, 301

SFFZY, GKZU VAFXUASY, AUIUKXU BOUKA
IOKUL XHGNU LAFD BOU YBHDV HRP
UYBUUD FL HJUY BOAFNJO MOKIO BOUC
OHXU VHYYUP.

351.

HINTS: 154, 310, 141

MGFZCFZWCFZ XH ZJSZ HZSZXGF XF DXLC
PJCF ZJC EGFCHCH JSOC S JSTB ZXWC
QCCKXFN YK PXZJ VGY.

352.

HINTS: 210, 65, 226

ZX CXO DXCKYCS HXFA DEYPZASC OX HXFA
XVC PSJACYCL KXA OESH VSAS IXAC YC
JCXOESA OYRS.

353.

HINTS: 23, 433, 158

GO UFXO KOHZ VM ZCO SYRH GCOM GO
KOUVOXO ZCYZ GO YUFMO UFXO, ZCYZ MF
FMO CYH OXOI UFXOS UVQO TH YMS MF
FMO OXOI GVUU.

354.

HINTS: 394, 471, 378

YBOF ZFBZTF QWAKL QWIQ EBOAKR QB
RSAZY GAQW TANF OFIKY WIKCYWILAKR
HBXS GIH QWSBXRW.

355.

HINTS: 224, 460, 16

F KIIG EFL UI ETGZQ IRU UAZ IHG
VUWFTKAU FQG QFWWIE JFUA EIRHG DZ OIW
CIWZ OIHMV UI EFHM IQ TU.

356.

HINTS: 278, 199, 329

RWVO ZSEYD HJEAJGJ AV EWB WVK SUKJU—
FUSGAKJK CNJO WUJ WEESBJK CS EWO KSBV
CNJ EWB WVK LAGJ CNJ SUKJUD.

357.

HINTS: 25, 241, 41

SGIRIZGYKY YVM KNC NLUVP YWCOGCY GY
ZCKKGPZ KVRRCH VRR KNC KGUC SLK YKGRR
OVP'K KCRR TNCHC GK'Y NCVFCF.

358.

HINTS: 11, 386, 332

QOKV QOVG QOUG QOV, QOMKAR

QOJWKQDAKOU QGAOEG DI LGWHGUI.

QOUG QOVG QOKV QOVVGW, QGHHKAR LGW

QOJWKQDAKOU TUOAH. QKHH QKHHGH

NGEDQKAR QKHHSH.

359.

HINTS: 404, 107, 436

YKXMJMHXMS YKXYJUXQMHX IUHMOTH

WYQOTUXXU GMXD QYHU-XMTXUI WUTH EYQ

CMUGMTO SZQQUTX GYQWI HRZLPPWUH.

360.

HINTS: 265, 442, 55

PRXPDXOBNOD NJJ WRYB OQRYKQOL YTRX

OQD GRBM NO QNXC. OQD LYX'L BNWL CR

XRO IYBX YXOUJ IBRYKQO OR N SRPYL.

361.

HINTS: 360, 110, 344

YUJTYCYARWV CSU QAZU XCSFCAWV. PRM

WUHUS ZWRG NRG XCLQP PRM CSU XUAWF

VYMWF MWYAQ CBYUS PRM NCHU BCQQUW

BRS YNUJ.

362. HINTS: 317, 389, 418

AQWU UXFVL XRI XKYYZ ZRQ'C PG FJ ZRQ

TRWU GNGHZUXFVM ZRQ XKNG HFMXU VRI—

KVC UXGV MRU FU PKBL KMKFV.

363. HINTS: 1, 117, 220

QUJJDY ZBJ MPPX FPADXPF BJ KZP BSK UA

JBCDXQ XUKZDXQ DX B RBC KZBK OPBLPJ

YSBVKDVBOOC XUKZDXQ NXJBDF.

364. HINTS: 9, 118, 353

TPRRBTT JT L DULPX LDOBU LHH. YN OVB

OJGB NEP'UB UJRV BAEPCV OE THBBQ HLOB

NEP'UB TE EHX NEP LHMLNT MLZB PQ

BLUHN.

365. HINTS: 310, 210, 473

XTTXAWGFCWP VXDKF'W ZFXBZ WRDKD VIPK;

CW ACFEK WRD TRXFD IFV IKZK I KCOOP

MGDKWCXF.

366. HINTS: 237, 222, 365

V FSKZOT FQAHFTN AH V ZNSOW SU QSNBH

VKB WJNVHTH QJAIJ ZTFH CSON FVKZ VYY

FSKZOTYTB OW.

367. HINTS: 422, 163, 218

X LRP LAWRDAK X DXQ MIAQ IA MXNHK

XERGQV X CGVVNA RZ MXFAE BQKFAXV RZ

FIERGJI BF.

368. HINTS: 242, 472, 229

G RDOWJ TEIPLT CGI DK E FOHFVGK EKJ

PEYL GI EWW ID HUCLWM IPEK ID XL

BTDRJLJ DK E YLWYLI BOCPGDK. —IPDTLEO

1. It is unwise to complain loudly about how the ball bounces, especially if you are the one who dropped it.

2. Do you know that William Taft was the first president to make regular use of an automobile while he was chief executive?

3. The worst inhumanity we can show our fellow creatures is to be completely indifferent to their needs.

4. People who try to make an impression often do; it is often not the kind of impression they try to make.

5. Slick deadbeat, wanting to pay his bill with a check, was told by waiter that management rules require paying check with a bill.

6. The wise fellow could find great consolation in nearly anything; smaller salary means smaller taxes.

7. About the only thing that goes as far today as it did ten years ago is the dime that rolls under the bed.

8. When you stretch towards the stars, you may not reach one, but you will not end up with a handful of mud, either.

9. A real leader is one who can guess which way the crowd will be going and then get out in front.

10. You could get the short end of the bargain if you should decide to trade opportunity for security.

11. There are very few errors made by a mother-in-law who is an ever-willing babysitter.

12. What a pity that people who have closed minds usually don't have mouths to match.

13. With modern jet planes, it is entirely possible to enjoy dinner in America and have heartburn over Europe.

14. Holding a grudge is similar to having a burr in your shoe, which causes every step to be painful without shortening the trip.

15. When a young boy takes a bath of his own accord, it is a sure thing he is going on his first date.

16. Even if money grew on trees, some people would have to write home between harvests for some dough.

17. Modern man is fellow who drives mortgaged car over bond-financed highway on credit card gasoline.

18. Speaker's fervent prayer: "Fill my mouth with proper stuff, and nudge me when I have said enough."

19. Four "imps" very often cause accidents: improvising, impatience, impunity, and impulsiveness.

20. Capable cop chases, catches callous criminal; first cumbersome confession closes case.

21. Remedy for frustration caused by high bill from doctor: Think of what an undertaker would charge.

22. Beauteous blonde, bewitched by big, bright bankroll, banishes best, but broke, beau; becomes banker's bride.

23. A young lady returned a dictionary to the library with the comment, "It's too disconnected to be interesting."

24. They will have reached adolescence when a boy notices that a girl notices that he is noticing her.

25. Wondering child gravely asked mother if condensed milk comes from very short cows.

26. Some plan must be devised immediately to prevent organized crime from disorganizing society.

27. Smart-aleck teenager ribbed his parents by asking if they used to ride to school on the bumpy backs of dinosaurs.

28. When dressing a fidgety baby, merely get hold of a button, then wait until the buttonhole comes around.

29. What were previously called television station breaks are now more often like compound fractures.

30. For each hour the average person drives his car, or is tied up in traffic, he leaves it parked for eleven hours.

31. It seems each person you meet can prescribe a cure for the common cold—but not your doctor.

32. Our next-door neighbor says his domestic explosion appears to have been touched off by an old flame.

33. Try not to find very much wrong with your children. Perhaps they have patterned themselves after you.

34. One town, unable to afford radar but wishing to cut down on speeders, hung up this road sign: "Speed Trap Ahead."

35. The fellow who first said "a penny for your thoughts" had evidently never paid for psychoanalysis.

36. Humor is something like a needle and thread, for, if deftly used, it can patch up practically anything.

37. Despite the calendar, the very shortest night of the year is Christmas Eve—from sundown to son-up.

38. Anger is a potent acid that does more harm to that in which it is stored than it can to that on which it is poured.

39. Remember, an elevator operator might have his ups and downs, but he is one of the few people who knows where he is going.

40. The average person would much prefer to be complimented for a youthful appearance than praised for wisdom attributed to age.

41. Pedestrian: fellow who was so sure there were still a couple of gallons of gas in the car.

42. The wonder of a single snowflake far outweighs the wisdom of a whole universe of meteorologists.

43. An optimist is a person who is sure he has heard all of the humorous definitions of an optimist.

44. You are only human if your mind wanders, but the trouble comes when you start to follow it.

45. Many men, like thermometers, are influenced by conditions surrounding them; the others, like thermostats, do something about it.

46. Cryptologist constructed some very difficult cryptograms and stumped nearly all solvers.

47. The good old days—when a teenager went into the garage and came out pushing the lawn mower.

48. To have all that you want may be riches; however, to be completely content with your lot is wealth.

49. Diplomat—one who has the ability to take something, and yet make the other person believe he is giving it away.

50. Despite what people say, very few folks have more money than they know what to do with.

51. Making speeches is usually like spelling Mississippi; you must know when to stop.

52. Why do many children seem to eat their spinach in slow motion—inach by inach?

53. You have arrived socially when you can successfully hold a cocktail and plate of canapés and carry on a conversation with only two hands.

54. Maybe they call it modern art because it may not be around long enough to be called anything else.

55. Mabel, upon receiving word via cable that she won coat of sable with famous Paris label, started dancing atop table.

56. Lumberjack, named Jackie Black, got pretty lucky and won himself stack of jack while playing blackjack.

57. Remember, the dictionary is the only place where you'll find success comes before work.

58. Try to learn from the mistakes of others. You will not live long enough to make them all yourself.

59. Think how much a mother kangaroo must dislike a rainy day when the kids cannot play outside.

60. The reason the dog is man's best pal is probably because he never gives advice, borrows money, or has in-laws.

61. Money may not be everything—however, it has a pretty good lead over whatever is in second place.

62. Schedule all your worrying for a specific half-hour around the middle of the day. Then take a nap during this period.

63. Specialist: doctor whose patients are well enough trained to call on him only during daylight hours.

64. Science has yet to discover why the ones who want to get off on the second floor are always in the rear of the elevator.

65. Spring is the season when the birds you fed all winter repay you by eating your newly planted grass seed.

66. Whenever a fellow makes a mistake, at least it proves he stopped talking and tried to do something.

67. A modern pioneer is a mother of four youngsters who survives a rainy weekend when the television is not working.

68. It is not enough merely to possess a fine aim in life; it is also necessary for you to pull the trigger.

69. The safest method to use to double your money is to fold it once and put it back in your pocket.

70. If you can make one person happy every day, in forty years you have contributed to the happiness of almost fifteen thousand people.

71. Some people never appear to have an opinion—they use one that happens to be in style at the time.

72. Note to Boy Scouts—the fastest way known to make a fire with two sticks is to make sure one of them is a match.

73. If your problems seem endless, remember a diamond is but a piece of coal that has been hard-pressed for many years.

74. All any firm asks of a new employee is that he be fifty percent of what he claimed to be the day he applied for the position.

75. The principal difference between psychoneurosis and plain nervousness is about one hundred and fifty dollars.

76. Withholding tax is an ingenious system for preventing the taxpayer from getting warmly attached to his money.

77. It is practically impossible to be a top dog, especially if you spend all of your spare time growling.

78. Most speakers state that it takes up to three weeks to prepare a proper impromptu speech.

79. The United States Constitution was not drawn up until eleven years after the signing of the Declaration of Independence.

80. Passport photographs usually make folks look as if they were emerging dolefully from a lost weekend.

81. If you should ever have the feeling that you are being sadly neglected, remember Whistler's father.

82. If you would like to see a model home, you should learn what time she is through work.

83. A small boy glumly objected to going to school since he could not read, could not write, and was not allowed to talk.

84. The first day of spring and the first real spring day are often as much as a month apart.

85. An onion can make folks cry, but nobody has yet invented a vegetable that can cause them to laugh.

86. An old Spanish saying: "It is very nice to do nothing all day—then have the night to rest up."

87. One good way to test your memory is to try to remember the things that worried you yesterday.

88. "The chief function of the body is to carry the brain around," said Thomas A. Edison.

89. Those who eavesdrop hear nothing good about themselves—but sure learn who their pals are.

90. Perhaps it is better to appreciate what one cannot own than to own what one cannot appreciate.

91. Overconfidence is that certain feeling that folks have when they don't know what they are getting into.

92. All an argument amounts to is two or more people attempting hard to get in the last word first.

93. "No man is good enough to govern another man without that other man's consent," said Lincoln.

94. By the time you have your child suited, scarved, and booted, snapped, mittened, and belted, the snow has melted.

95. You know youngsters are really growing up when they start asking questions that have logical answers.

96. A compromise is often an agreement between two people, each of whom ends up with something he does not actually want.

97. Even if you have all the answers, you may not be able to sift the right ones from the wrong ones.

98. Many a romance that started beside a waterfall at a summer resort has ended beside a leaky faucet in the kitchen sink.

99. The prime essentials for happiness in life are something to do, something to love, and something to hope for.

100. A cynic is a person who knows the price of everything, yet knows the actual value of nothing.

101. There is something much nicer than receiving praise—the feeling of having earned it.

102. Many men of a timid nature prefer the comparative calm of despotism to the boisterous ocean of liberty.

103. To maintain a well-balanced perspective, each man who owns a dog that worships him should also have a cat to ignore him.

104. Perfect timing is attained when one can turn off the hot and cold water faucets in the shower simultaneously.

105. Modern children who constantly play hooky could well be called "unlicensed curriculum abstainers."

106. There must be a better place for four people to be miserable together than at the bridge table.

107. No advice is entirely without value, because even a watch that does not run is correct twice daily.

108. The best things in life are free, so they say, but is it not a pity that the next-best things are so very expensive?

109. Conduct yourself so that you could calmly sell the family parrot to your town's worst gossip.

110. If you can arise cheerfully on a very cold morning, it is a matter of mind over mattress.

111. Optimism: a cheerful frame of mind such as allows a teakettle to sing though in hot water up to its nose.

112. If you are able to make people think they need an item they have never even heard of before, you are truly a salesman.

113. A gentleman is one who won't stare at a girl in a bathing suit unless he is wearing sunglasses.

114. There is only one really pretty child in the hospital nursery, and each mother possesses it.

115. August is the month when the mate to that argyle sock you received in winter for Christmas is finally finished.

116. May all your woes in the New Year be of as brief duration as most of your New Year's resolutions.

117. A pessimist is one man who feels bad when he feels good for fear he'll feel worse when he feels better.

118. That condition which in the subway is called congestion is termed "intimacy" in our best nightclubs.

119. Formal ceremony is the invention of very wise men to make dolts keep their distance.

120. The most important thing about a problem is not its solution but the strength gained in finding the solution.

121. By the time you finally reach greener pastures, you can often no longer climb the fence.

122. Remember when you got any repairs done by the landlord by simply threatening to move out?

123. A husband I know is terribly careless about his appearance; he hasn't shown up in years.

124. Whoever said, "A work you've done well never needs doing over," evidently never pulled weeds in the garden.

125. It is not possible for people whose fists are tightly clenched to offer others a friendly handclasp.

126. The peaceful dew is the silent tears of the night that fall as it weeps softly for joy at seeing all the wonderful creations of the day.

127. According to recent fashion trends you may well expect to find the suitless swimming strap next year.

128. Folks who claim to say what they think are often doing more saying than thinking.

129. Book reviewer most likely is one fellow who makes his living by the sweat of his browse.

130. Happiness is that peculiar elated sensation you get when you are much too busy to be bothered worrying.

131. A sure sign that your heart is strong is being able to watch a parking attendant park your brand-new car.

132. It is truly annoying the way some people keep right on talking when you are trying to interrupt.

133. Trouble with many of the part-time workers is they are employed on full-time basis.

134. It is fairly easy to discover the genuine egotist in a group—he is the fellow me-deep in conversation.

135. A really happy home is a lot more than a roof over your head—it is a very firm foundation under your feet.

136. Why does a true story need to change hands but a few times to become fiction?

137. You reach full maturity the minute keeping a secret is much more satisfying than passing it along.

138. A certain amount of character is lost the moment a high ideal is sacrificed to conformity and popularity.

139. Most well-adjusted people are able to play golf or bridge as though they are just games.

140. Faith is knowing and believing the sun is shining, even when the sky is full of black clouds.

141. Opportunities can be completely missed because we are busy broadcasting when we ought to be tuning in.

142. One good way to prevent troubled thoughts from ever entering your mind is to have something far better inside it.

143. A furtive whisper is one way to make many folks believe what they probably otherwise wouldn't.

144. If the gravy is hot enough, there'll not be many complaints about lack of flavor.

145. My best friend found plastic surgery can do almost anything except keep nose out of other people's business.

146. One of the newest outlying shopping centers covers so much ground it has even considered applying for statehood.

147. The one thing far more difficult than following a strict regimen of any type is not imposing it on others.

148. When the world began, a pink blob of sunset fell from the sky into a pool of blue water and made the flamingo.

149. Diplomat—man who can keep his shirt on while getting something off his chest.

150. If asked for information, one should not make mistake of going further and including advice.

151. Individual who did much to arouse working class was alarm clock inventor.

152. Any speaker who has not struck oil in twenty minutes ought to stop boring immediately.

153. Artist has it over photographer; he can paint countryside and leave out the billboards.

154. The gate to wisdom swings easiest on hinges of common sense and uncommon ideas.

155. Child's apt description of a peacock seen for the first time—chicken in full bloom.

156. Why does wood burn so easily in the forest and with such difficulty in our fireplace?

157. Before you decide to argue with the boss, it is a good idea to look carefully at two sides—his side, and the outside.

158. Mind not the man who belittles you, because he is simply hoping to cut you down to his own size.

159. You can give the egotist much credit because he very seldom talks about other people.

160. Trouble with this life—one is halfway finished before he catches on it is do-it-yourself job.

161. Nothing can break up a discussion as fast as a fellow who knows what he is talking about.

162. Most of our problems would resolve themselves if we forgot them and went fishing.

163. Next to being shot at and missed, is anything so satisfying as refund on your income tax?

164. All too often the person who thinks that he is pretty hot turns out to be only half-baked.

165. It is most important that all great ideas have landing gear as well as wings.

166. It is most difficult for a person to make for himself a place in the sun if he constantly seeks refuge under the family tree.

167. It may be that the only time many of us do not "pass the buck" is if a collection is taken up.

168. Maybe they call it take-home pay because there is no other place you can go on it!

169. Nobody has been known to get eyestrain from looking on the bright side of life.

170. Very often it takes only a good wife to make an old rake into a lawn mower.

171. Although education covers a lot of ground, it does not necessarily cultivate it.

172. Franklin may have discovered electricity; however, the fellow who invented meters made more money.

173. Lovely autumn—the season that washes with cool, fresh dew the dusty face of summer.

174. The true path to happiness comes from completely losing yourself in a cause much greater than yourself.

175. It's really not hard to spot a fool unless you find he's hiding inside you.

176. My pet dog and I show the very same good taste in selecting slippers—what I choose, he chews too.

177. There should be a musical instrument in each home except the one next door.

178. A group of folks that keeps "minutes" and wastes hours is called a committee.

179. Shoes are usually bought by men to fit their feet while women buy them to fit the occasion.

180. The fellow who paddles his own canoe doesn't have to wait for his ship to come in.

181. Almost every child you know would learn to write sooner if allowed to do his homework on wet cement.

182. It is absolutely impossible to put footprints in the sands of time if you are always sitting down.

183. Sometimes we tend to forget that anger is, after all, merely one letter short of danger.

184. Many young couples feel that if they postpone payment until a future date it is not really spending.

185. An obstacle is what you see when you lift your eyes off the goal you are trying to reach.

186. Like most vehicles, the cost of operating a grocery cart at the supermarket goes up with every stop.

187. Snow and adolescence are two big problems that will eventually disappear if you can only ignore them long enough.

188. I took five remedies for my recent cold and I swiftly recovered; now I want to know which one did the trick.

189. During this age of progress it really seems strange no one has found satisfactory replacements for safety pins.

190. Keeping house: a lot like stringing a strand of pearls without a knot at the end of the string.

191. Nothing is more effective for putting humans in good mood than undeserved praise.

192. A lecture can give you the feeling of being numb on one end and dumb on the other.

193. Don't blithely expect to grow big if inclined to shrink away from any kind of responsibility.

194. Every generation laughs heartily at old fashions and avidly follows new.

195. You cannot buy the best advertising—for it is written on the wagging tongues of satisfied customers.

196. Punctuality is the art of guessing precisely how late the other guy will be.

197. The secret of the word "triumph" is completely contained within its first syllable.

198. One cannot be very bright if he decides nest eggs are only for the birds.

199. A child rarely learns how educational his newest toy really is until his dad trips over it.

200. When you feel dog-tired at night, it may be because you growled all day.

201. Hardest thing for some people to say in twenty-five words or less is "goodbye."

202. No one should spend so much time preparing for a rainy day that he forgets to appreciate the sunshine.

203. He that teaches his child to be thrifty and economical has already bequeathed him a fortune.

204. It's very nice to see people with a lot of get-up-and-go—especially if they're visiting you.

205. Your best friend's new mink stole can suddenly make you feel terribly poor.

206. Dandelions are much like some humans—given an inch they will take over a yard.

207. We must admit that science is resourceful, for when it could not open the window it air-conditioned the train.

208. Differing from growing things—voices which are cultivated should never be raised.

209. Why not teach your children that the easiest way to rid themselves of an unwelcome chore is to do it immediately.

210. Training means learning the rules; experience means learning the exceptions to them.

211. Formula for success: Think up a product that costs a dime to make, sells for a dollar, and is habit-forming.

212. Beware of a half-truth for you may find you grabbed hold of the wrong half.

213. One remarkable thing is the way absence can make the heart grow fonder of somebody else.

214. Bad habits are similar to a comfortable bed—easy enough to get into, but terribly difficult to get out of.

215. Practicing the golden rule is never a sacrifice—it should be thought of as a long-term investment.

216. Do something every day to make other people happy even if it is only leaving them alone.

217. Just when you've got the shape for the job, your children stop believing in Santa Claus.

218. Success is a bright, glowing sun that makes ridiculously unimportant all the shadowy flecks of many failures.

219. Moral courage is when you are positive a course of action is right, then follow it despite adverse criticism.

220. There could assuredly be a much greater volume of work turned out if we did not live in such a "clock-eyed" world.

221. With the constant cost of living rise, it is hard to feel sure that what goes up must come down.

222. What we call "discretion" in humans might be termed "cunning" in animals.

223. Most of us fail to put our best foot forward until we find the other one in hot water.

224. It takes only a small stream to carry a lot of water to the ocean—if it keeps right on going.

225. For a very beguiling conversation it actually takes three people—two to talk, with one to be the topic.

226. A truly educated man is one whose thorough academic knowledge matures into wisdom.

227. Experience, though often expensive and dangerous, is still an excellent teacher.

228. If you can cross a lawn without stopping to pull a weed, chances are the property is not yours.

229. Many a talent can be completely wasted because it is not properly harnessed.

230. Experience is the exact alphabet needed for reading life's most important messages.

231. It is astounding how big a part ignorance can play in causing some people to be completely satisfied with themselves.

232. If you often are pushed by someone behind you, then you must be out in front.

233. Water and words—simple to pour, but impossible to recover, once poured.

234. Suspicion is nothing but a mental picture seen through a completely imaginary keyhole.

235. Airplanes with pontoons look a little like dragonflies wearing galoshes.

236. The only difference between a modern artist and a child is that the child will probably improve.

237. Youth is that period in life which the young ones are hoping to grow out of, and the old ones are hoping to recapture.

238. Poets that prate about autumn leaves very obviously possess no eaves.

239. Charm is a way of getting the answer "yes" without actually asking anything clearly.

240. Upon arising in the morning the rest of the day often depends entirely on our rest of the night.

241. Cheerfulness is the principal ingredient in the prescription for good health.

242. Old-timer: one who remembers when a twist was something added to a highball.

243. A very poor memory is a most effective defense against spreading gossip.

244. Employees are valuable in proportion to their ability to work harmoniously with others.

245. How come some office employees are so efficient at nail filing, yet so poor at mail filing?

246. To be popular you must endure being taught many things you already know.

247. A grapefruit may be yellow, but you must admit it rarely fails to strike back if it's attacked.

248. Fish story: If you go around with your mouth open wide, you may get hooked.

249. Trouble is one thing that defies the law of gravity because it is usually far easier to pick up than to drop.

250. It is unnecessary for you to be in a key position before you are able to unlock the door of opportunity.

251. A lot of babies are spoiled because too few parents have the nerve to chastise two doting grandpas.

252. For every person who thinks profoundly, a hundred more are moved by nothing but force or feeling.

253. We may have committed the golden rule to memory; now let us commit it to living.

254. We really should not worry about our adolescents—because our parents worried about us and what good did it do?

255. When alone, guard your thoughts; with your family, guard your temper; and with friends, guard your words.

256. When you shut your eyes to temptation, better be sure you don't make it look like a wink.

257. Many alarm clocks are practically useless; especially those within arm's reach.

258. It is often much easier to fight for our principles than to live up to them.

259. Life is similar to a radio comedy in that it does not always follow the script.

260. The amount of sleep needed by the average person is usually a good five minutes more.

261. If you eat slowly, you usually eat less. This is always true if you are a member of a big family.

262. Poise is the art of getting what you want by raising your eyebrow instead of the roof.

263. The fastest possible way for you to start a fire is to rub two opposing opinions together.

264. Always hold your head erect, but be very careful to have your nose at a friendly level.

265. True wisdom is knowing precisely when to speak your mind, and when to mind your speech.

266. The most serious problem in the world might have been very easily solved when it was a small one.

267. If you want the world to beat a path to your front door, lie down to take a nap, or try to take a bath.

268. Surely the best education is that obtained endeavoring to earn a living.

269. Success is the attainment of what you want while you are still in the mood for it.

270. If the shoe fits, wear it—unless you are a woman. Then, of course, you will want a size smaller.

271. I have a hunch birds are generous—the dove brings peace, the stork brings tax exemptions.

272. Many folks who are positive are really mistaken at the top of their voices.

273. Your children are growing up when your daughter starts putting on lipstick and your son starts wiping it off.

274. Horseback riding makes you wonder how anything filled with hay could be so hard.

275. One possible advantage television has over a good book is that two people can curl up with it.

276. Dignity is possibly the one thing that cannot ever be preserved in alcohol.

277. If Mother Nature had known about Bermuda shorts she very likely would have done better with the male knee.

278. Americans rarely seem to care how much they must pay for something they want, as long as it is not all at once.

279. Perhaps what we really need in these extremely hectic days is a "calmplex."

280. A football coach's toughest problems are a good defensive team and offensive alumni.

281. Saint Bernard chases cat into curio shop; fine crockery, including costly china coffee cups, get chipped, cracked, busted.

282. The more cheerfulness and good humor that is used, the more of it remains.

283. You probably are a complete success if you own the tiniest car and the most powerful mower in the neighborhood.

284. Love may be only a chemical reaction, but it sure is fun trying to discover the right formula.

285. Our youngsters today have the disadvantage of having too many advantages.

286. Horse sense is seeing things as they are, but doing things as they ought to be done.

287. A good man is similar to tea—for his real strength shows when he finds himself in hot water.

288. Anyone is welcome to use our new lawn mower if they do not take it out of our backyard.

289. The most discouraging thing when you reach middle age is really all those years gone to waist.

290. The finest of all gifts around any Christmas tree— the presence of a glowing family all wrapped up in each other.

291. We find it is an impossibility for a person to begin to learn something he thinks he already knows.

292. No doubt you heard about the grim fellow who called his car "Flattery" because it got him nowhere.

293. "My boy is a bootblack, now," said the farmer to the city folks. "Yes sir, I make hay while the son shines."

294. The comfortable temperature of a home is usually maintained by the cool heads and warm hearts of those who dwell there.

295. A lost opportunity can seldom be retrieved because the chances are that some alert person has already discovered it.

296. In most young men's "salad days," perhaps the biggest problem was locating enough lettuce to go with the tomatoes.

297. Go-getter: A person who enters after you in a revolving door and winds up way ahead of you.

298. History, after all is said and done, is only gossip which happens to grow old gracefully.

299. Opportunity may knock; however, temptation usually kicks the door down.

300. A child's description of a hotel: A place you stay at if you have no relatives.

301. One wonderful thing about conformity—you may practice it without being conspicuous.

302. Newspaper ad: "Doughnut shop being put up for fast sale; owner in a big hole."

303. Fame and fortune will smile on the man who can contrive to invent tearproof onion peelers.

304. We find, if we remove four letters from the word "queue," we still pronounce it "Q." How peculiar!

305. Success isn't always final. If you build a better mousetrap, nature will breed a smarter mouse.

306. They say it is better, by far, to have loved a short fellow than never to have loved a tall.

307. From the time of a catch and the telling of it, a fish often increases amazingly in size.

308. Many people believe genius to be a hereditary thing; those who think otherwise must certainly have no children.

309. Too much dancing can affect the heart—and sitting out too many isn't good for it, either.

310. When Pop popped popcorn, it popped so hard that it popped into Pop's pocket, until Pop's pocket looked like a pocket that would pop.

311. Experience is a hard teacher. She's the only one who presents the test first and the lesson afterward.

312. Nothing makes us pay up past due dentist bills in great hurry like throbbing toothaches.

313. If you allow your kids to think money grows on trees, someday they could get caught out on a limb.

314. The reason many men lose an argument with an alarm clock is because they take it lying down.

315. It's a peculiar thing about life—if you absolutely refuse to accept anything but the best, you often get it.

316. By using a modern budget it's now possible for two people to go into debt systematically.

317. If you owe a lot, don't worry, for even the birds have bills and they're singing their hearts out.

318. Nowadays, the only thing important to put aside for one's old age is all thought of retirement.

319. When the fly fell into the marmalade jar he was overheard saying, "Just how did I ever get into this jam?"

320. Golf ball: Just a very small object which remains on the tee while a perspiring human fans it vigorously with a long club.

321. Set your goal high. You may not reach it, but you'll put on muscle climbing upward toward it.

322. It's humanly possible for a person to do a tremendous amount of labor—that is, if it's not the thing he's supposed to be doing.

323. Indulge in at least one hearty laugh each day. If nothing funnier comes along, laugh at yourself.

324. There is no reason to make the same mistake twice when there are so many others to make.

325. If you ask a child for the truth, find a handy chair to sink into. You will get it—and nine times out of ten it will floor you.

326. Obstacles are put in your path to find out whether you really wanted a certain thing or if you just thought you did.

327. To locate a parking place just circle the block and you'll usually see the car ahead pulling into it.

328. I never brag about the very big fish I catch, but still I see no reason for carrying them home through the alleys.

329. It's the kind of song you sing and the friendly smile you wear that makes the sunshine.

330. Culture is that which makes us think we will like something strange when we know we won't.

331. Big politicians who try to please everybody at once are like a pup trying to follow four kids at the same time.

332. Poise is the ability to talk brightly and fluently while the other fellow is paying the waiter.

333. Perhaps the dachshund becomes a good family dog because all the members of the family can pat him at the same time.

334. By observing the overcrowded melee of traffic nowadays it looks like all the former backseat drivers finally got their own cars.

335. Maturity, regardless of age, has been attained if a person does not judge, but simply learns to understand and enjoy people.

336. From child's prayer: "...and please, Lord, put vitamins in cherry pie and ice cream instead of cod-liver oil. Amen."

337. A lie is a pretty poor old substitute for the truth, but the only one so far discovered.

338. Some people seldom have their own opinions, they just wear whatever jumble happens to be in style.

339. It's remarkable how much fun you can get laughing at your own passport picture before realizing that's what you look like.

340. One perfect way to make a long story short is to start telling it meekly to a traffic cop.

341. There is a vast difference in being open-minded and having a perfectly empty hole in one's head.

342. A black cat following you is often bad luck depending upon whether you're a man or a mouse.

343. Revolutions are like earthquakes. If they overturn much that is faulty they destroy much that is good.

344. Great secret of social alchemy: Gather all life's leaves in spring, its flowers in summer, its fruit in autumn.

345. Charity never seems sweeter than when entered in exemptions column of income tax return.

346. Slalom skiing: zigzag down slope, around pylons, quick turn, reach final goal. First prize won.

347. Quarterback safely completes forty-yard dash, scoring winning touchdown for home team.

348. It is the common wonder of all men how among so many millions of faces there should be none alike.

349. According to researchers at Northwestern University, the Chicago fire was believed to have started in a riotous dice game.

350. Books, like proverbs, receive their chief value from the stamp and esteem of ages through which they have passed.

351. Contentment is that station in life when the Joneses have a hard time keeping up with you.

352. Do not confine your children to your own learning for they were born in another time.

353. We love best in the days when we believe that we alone love, that no one has ever loved like us and no one ever will.

354. Some people think that coming to grips with life means handshaking your way through.

355. A good way to widen out the old straight and narrow path would be for more folks to walk on it.

356. Many folks believe in law and order—provided they are allowed to lay down the law and give the orders.

357. Biologists say the human species is getting taller all the time but still can't tell where it's headed.

358. Maid made male mad, making matrimonial menace of herself. Male made maid madder, messing her matrimonial plans. Miss misses becoming missus.

359. Optimistic optometrist designs lorgnette with rose-tinted lens for viewing current world squabbles.

360. Concentrate all your thoughts upon the work at hand. The sun's rays do not burn until brought to a focus.

361. Temptations are like bargains. You never know how badly you are being stung until after you have fallen for them.

362. Just think how happy you'd be if you lost everything you have right now—and then got it back again.

363. Gossip has been defined as the art of saying nothing in a way that leaves practically nothing unsaid.

364. Success is a fraud after all. By the time you're rich enough to sleep late you're so old you always wake up early.

365. Opportunity doesn't knock these days; it rings the phone and asks a silly question.

366. A tongue twister is a group of words and phrases which gets your tang all tongueled up.

367. A boy becomes a man when he walks around a puddle of water instead of through it.

368. I would rather sit on a pumpkin and have it all to myself than to be crowded on a velvet cushion. —Thoreau